EFFECTIVE EVALUATION OF TRAINING AND DEVELOPMENT IN HIGHER EDUCATION

EFFECTIVE EVALUATION
OF TRAINING
AND DEVELOPMENT
IN HIGHER EDUCATION

Bob Thackwray

**KOGAN
PAGE**

London · Stirling (USA)

First published in 1997

Kogan Page Limited
120 Pentonville Road
London N1 9JN
and
22883 Quicksilver Drive
Stirling, VA 20166, USA

British Library Cataloguing in Publication Data
A CIP record for this book is available from the British Library.
ISBN 0 7494 2122 3

Typeset by Northern Phototypesetting Co Ltd, Bolton
Printed and bound in Great Britain by Clays Ltd, St Ives plc

Contents

CONTENTS

Acknowledgements

Particular thanks to members of the Universities' and Colleges' Staff Development Agency Task Force on Evaluation:
Richard Blackwell, University of Nottingham
Pam Fitsimmons, University of the West of England
Louise Harden, University of Newcastle at Northumbria
Mike Laycock, University of East London
Lin Thorley, University of Hertfordshire

Thanks to all those who offered case study material, suggestions, support and advice, including:

Melanie Armstrong, The Robert Gordon University
Lesley Bailey, HPC Industrial Products
Nigel Beasley, University of Leicester
Andrew Bewley, University of Teesside
Keith Burgess, Newnorth Print
Josè Chambers, King Alfred's College
Paul Dixon, The Open University
Ruth Goodall, University of East Anglia
David Gosling, University of East London
Penny Hatton, University of Leeds
Brian Hillier, The Assessment Network
Paul Hughes, Bristol University
Steve Ketteridge, Queen Mary and Westhill College
John Marincowitz, Queen Elizabeth's School
Phil McMenemy, Gateshead College
Tony Miller, Liverpool Victoria Friendly Society
Chris Moore, Gateshead College
Jennie Merriman, Sheffield Hallam University
Rebecca Nestor, University of Oxford

ACKNOWLEDGEMENTS

Doug Rogers, HPC Industrial Products
Pete Sayers, University of Bradford
Melissa Shaw, University of Central Lancashire
Patrick Smith, Buckinghamshire College
Pat Stewart, The Industrial Society
Stan Taylor, University of Newcastle
Peter Taylor, Senior Assessor (Investors in People) and Independent Consultant
Annie Tillson, Audit and Financial Services, Northamptonshire County Council
Special thanks to Professor Gus Pennington for his invaluable comments on the first draft. Thanks also to Pat Lomax of Kogan Page for encouragement, lunch and stress, (but not necessarily in that order).

Introduction

Tempora mutantur, et nos mutamur in illis
Times change and we change with them

'If training and development has value for the organisation it can be evaluated.'

Jackson in *Evaluation: Relating Training to Business Performance*, Kogan Page, 1989.

Is staff development of value? If it is, then it can – and must – be evaluated. In this book, some thoughts and reflections on the nature, structure and function of the evaluation of staff training and development are offered, with a focus on UK higher education.

Virtually all higher education institutions 'extol their support for staff development' (Barnett, 1992). Very few in practice can actually demonstrate the value of the investment they make, nor indeed can many agree on what they actually include under the potentially broad umbrella of training and development.

A range of approaches, techniques and instruments relating to the evaluation of training and development drawn from a variety of sources are presented and discussed in a higher education context. The related existing strengths of the sector are explored, notably with regard to teaching and learning and forms of quality assessment. Some references are made to external standards, in particular the Investors in People national standard which has done so much to bring effective evaluation of training and development more to the centre of the organisational stage.

An overarching theme, returned to time and again from a variety of perspectives is that, as a sector, higher education does not make full use of the knowledge and skills it already possesses in this area. A look back at some of the guidance from such bodies as the Council for National Academic Awards (CNAA) confirms this. For example:

The self evaluation exercise should seek to demonstrate the existence within the institution of a self critical academic community, able to reflect critically on its practice and on the results of evaluation. The following contextual matters should be taken into account:

1. the institution's mission statement and aims and corporate strategy;
2. the response made within the institution to changes in the higher education environment, notably an increased pressure on resources, any need to respond rapidly and flexibly to market forces, and any demands for widening access and expanding student numbers;
3. information already given to professional and other external agencies on an annual or periodic basis.

In common with other aspects of the management of academic quality and standards, the involvement of a peer review group will only be effective if, *inter alia*, it is properly briefed and given clearly defined objectives. Those should include:

1. ascertaining the institution's commitment to high quality at all levels;
2. examining the institution's basis for judging the quality of its courses;
3. considering the ways in which the institution provides conditions under which quality can be sustained and enhanced;
4. exploring the ways in which the institution has responded to the contextual issues described above.

The Management of Academic Quality in Institutions of Higher Education, CNAA, 1992

There are, or ought to be, particular 'bespoke systems of effective evaluation'; not just for higher education *per se* but for the institutions, faculties and departments that comprise the sector. Underpinning this assertion are formal and informal interviews and discussions with a wide variety of staff working in a wide variety of higher education institutions. On the one hand is the view that 'nothing happens except the happy sheet and a bit of number crunching' and on the other hand are the 'rigorous systems of validation and review, audit and assessment' and various other strategies evaluating teaching and learning that very often do not appear to figure in institutional or departmental calculations of the *real* benefits of training and development.

Senior managers, staff developers and indeed all those with responsibility for managing people and/or a budget most certainly need to know the 'tools of the trade' such as cost benefit, return on investment and payback. It is also essential to know whether they are appropriate for a particular institution, or for a particular evaluation (Jurans' 'fitness for purpose'). I will be suggesting that an appropriate model combines the strengths of the 'pay forward model' (see Chapter 5) and the flexibility and political sense of the 'responsive approach' to evaluation (see Chapter 4) set in the context of existing systems developed *by* higher education *for* higher education.

An old cliché asserts that to 'define is to limit'. Maybe so, but effective evaluation depends on sharp, clear and agreed parameters agreed in advance. This is not to argue that everyone should be singing from the same hymn sheet, but at least we should all know where the church is.

The evaluation of an activity seeks to measure some form of change. There are several areas where change due to training and development actions may be measured. These include:

- financial
- attitudinal
- behavioural
- functional (ie, effectiveness in performing duties/role/function)
- cognitive
- technical/skill

This is not an exhaustive nor exclusive list and it can be refined and added to. There are, in addition, many areas of overlap.

To set the scene it may be helpful to start with some definitions. It is without doubt an essential exercise for every organisation to have its own definition of training and development, a definition it has reached by consultation and discussion with staff at all levels. The list of definitions offered, therefore, is intended only to serve as a starting point or prompt for discussion, hence the multiple definitions in some instances.

Staff Development includes: 'everything that is done by and for staff in order to maintain and extend their work-related knowledge, skills and capabilities.' (University of Hertfordshire, 1996)

'the institutional policies, programmes and procedures which facilitate and support staff so that they may fully serve their own and their institution's needs.' (Webb, 1996)

'the acquisition of knowledge, skills and experience which will aid personal development and underpin the University's future development.' (University of the West of England)

(Some higher education institutions define staff development by describing those activities that qualify for some form of support. The University of Northumbria at Newcastle does this and the definition is included in Chapter 12.)

Development is: 'the systematic development of the attitude/knowledge/skill/behaviour pattern required by an individual to perform adequately a given task or job.' (Department of Employment, 1981)

'any organisationally initiated procedures which are intended to foster learning among organisational members in a direction contributing to organisational effectiveness.' (Hinrichs, 1976)

'a set of management tools [where] the investment is made for the future performance of the organisation and is connected to organisational objectives for the future. The tools are used to enhance the skills and abilities which the individual needs to be able to move with the organisation and to pursue a career in line with its evolving needs.' (Jackson, 1989)

Training comprises: 'techniques aimed at improving what the organisation is doing by improving the skills of individuals and teams'.

'a set of management tools with the function of improving an organisation's current performance in terms of efficiency, effectiveness and productivity. The tools are used to develop skills and knowledge as a means of increasing individual, operational and organisational performance.' (Jackson, 1989)

(**Note:** Training and development are often grouped together and used interchangeably. This is wrong. They have different meanings. See Development and Staff Development.)

Evaluation is: '1. To ascertain or set the amount or value of.

2. To judge or assess the worth of.' (Collins Concise English Dictionary)

'the systematic collection of descriptive and judgmental information necessary to make effective decisions related to the selection, adoption, value and modification of various instructional activities.' (Goldstein, 1993)

'finding out and agreeing if what you are doing is worth doing, if you are doing it well and how you can do it better.' (Thackwray, 1996)

Efficiency is: the optimum use of all resources. An efficiency *gain* is providing the same service with fewer resources (ie, cost savings).

Effectiveness is: an output measure. *Increased* effectiveness is providing a better service with the same resources (ie, increased benefits)

Productivity: gains relate to providing a better service with less resources (ie, cost savings and increased benefits, in other words, the current situation of UK higher education).

Targets normally refer to *quantity*, eg 'to increase the number of publications'.

Standards normally refer to *quality* eg 'to be able to produce financial forecasts to 100% 'to increase the level of refereed journals'.

Quality

Effective evaluation is the significant contributor to quality control, quality assurance and quality enhancement. Beneath that rather glib assertion lies the often asked question: what *is* quality? There is no shortage of people ready to define quality and no shortage of definitions. Here is a small collection of some of them.

INTRODUCTION

Quality is:
- 'the totality of features and characteristics of a product or service which bear on its ability to satisfy stated or implied needs ... a predictable degree of uniformity and dependability, at low cost and suited to the market' (Deming, 1986)
- fitness for use (Juran, 1988)
- conformance to requirements (Crosby, 1984)
- the (minimum) loss imparted by the product to society from the time the product is shipped (Taguchi, 1985)
- in its essence a way of managing the organisation (Feigenbaum, 1986)
- correcting and preventing loss, not living with loss (Hoshin)
- the totality of features and characteristics of a product, service or process which bear on its ability to satisfy a given need from the customers point of view.' (British Standard Definition – substitute your own words for product and customer!)

With appropriate 'translation' all definitions have import for higher education especially, perhaps, Hoshin. ('Loss' in this context is not only limited to financial measures.)

Quality and Higher Education

1. The Academic Audit Unit (AAU)
The AAU was established in 1990. It was the forerunner of the Higher Education Quality Council (see 3 below). It described quality assurance as: 'the process by which those with institutional responsibility for quality can be sure that they know whether or not students are being given appropriate teaching and learning support and are reaching appropriate standards.'

2. Burge and Tannock
The quality of education is described as: 'the success with which an institution provides educational environments which enable students effectively to achieve worthwhile learning goals, including appropriate academic standards' (Burge and Tannock, 1994).

3. The UK Higher Education Quality Council (HEQC)
The *Guidelines on Quality Assurance* (p 11, 1996), in the section entitled Concepts of Quality offers the following by way of a higher education gloss on quality and its meaning:

'there are many different understandings of the term 'quality', often reflecting the interests of different constituencies in higher education. The guidelines cannot and do not prescribe any single overall model or approach to quality to which an institution is asked to adhere. Rather, they encompass the activities through which an institution satisfies itself that the quality of its educational provision is being maintained and that its standards are being met. 'Quality' is used here to refer to the range of a student's experience of higher education, while 'standards' refers

5

specifically to the levels of achievement that are expected and attained by students in their studies. Quality assurance is the means through which an institution confirms that the conditions are in place for students to achieve the standards set by the institution. Quality control provides the detailed procedures to render these conditions effective. A good system for quality assurance should meet its desired objectives without unnecessary bureaucracy or intrusion into an institution's primary activities.'

Perhaps the last word on quality should be left to Pirsig (1974) in *Zen And The Art Of Motorcycle Maintenance*:

'A real understanding of quality doesn't just serve the system, or even beat it or even escape it. A real understanding of quality captures the system, tames it, and puts it to work for one's own personal use, while leaving one completely free to pursue his own inner destiny.'

Assessment

As applied to students, a useful definition is: 'a systematic basis for making inferences about the learning and development of students … the process of defining, selecting, designing, collecting, analysing, interpreting and using information to increase students' learning and development.' (Erwin, 1991).

Validation

Higher education is, of course, very familiar with the process of validation and review. There is sometimes confusion as to the difference between validation and evaluation. Validation is a more limited process than evaluation. It acts as a checking mechanism. In the case of course or programme validation, it is checking that appropriate processes, practices and procedures have been observed to an agreed standard. In the case of training and development actions, validation simply serves to check that what was expected to happen has happened in the way it was intended to happen.

It should also be noted that a major area of confusion within most higher education institutions is that of the communication, or, more correctly, lack of communication, between 'academic' systems and 'personnel' systems. In the main this relates to the often inappropriate introduction and adoption of techniques and strategies originally designed for instructional training. Often, these models are introduced by staff in training and development sections of universities and colleges who previously had no experience of working in higher education. Equally, there is the reluctance of much of the academic community to recognise the value – even necessity – of some of these strategies. I have discussed and explored this with staff in both 'camps' in many universities and colleges of higher education.

In essence, there is one key message: *all* techniques and strategies have their place and value if used in the *right place* at the *right time* with the *right language* and, critically, using *existing skills, capabilities and attitudes* as the starting point. Knowing *how* and *when* to use them is the real challenge.

Finally, a word of warning. There are a number of roles ascribed to evaluation and by inference to evaluators. Some have negative connotations and the postholders tend to become insecure and destabilised. These roles include policing, spying, number crunching, acting as a management lackey and/or a bureaucrat. How the role is presented and subsequently managed is of paramount importance to the success and validity of the activity. Successful roles include internal consultant, troubleshooter, supporter, enabler and facilitator.

Section 1 Perspectives

Chapter 1

Evaluation and Higher Education

'Realisation of the vision for higher education that we have developed throughout our report is wholly dependent on the people in higher education. ... higher education should be able to recruit, retain and motivate staff of the appropriate calibre. ... an effective, fairly remunerated, professional and well–motivated workforce lies at the heart of the high quality system of higher education which this country will continue to need.'

NCIHE Report (1997) *Higher Education In The Learning Society. Report of the Committee,* Chapter 14, Staff In Higher Education

'As one who has spent his entire life, man, boy and raving old dotard, in and out of educational establishments I am the last person to offer any useful advice about them. Better leave that to politicians with no education, sense or commitment. They at least can bring an empty mind to the problem.'

Stephen Fry in *Paperweight*

The processes of evaluation within higher education have historically not been focused on the staff. This is especially true with regard to the teaching staff, and even more so when the development in question relates to aspects of teaching, learning and assessment that do not overtly relate to subject disciplines. Where there have been attempts they have mainly been haphazard, short term and not linked either clearly, or at all, to institutional or departmental objectives.

This is *not* an exercise concerning the development of new and cumbersome bureaucratic systems. The skills, knowledge and expertise have long existed within the sector. They are just focused elsewhere. Neither is this an attempt to promote the evaluation of *everything*. As is the case with staff development and training generally, *more* does *not* mean *better*. Most evaluations are a waste of time unless they start by clarifying the purpose they are intended to serve, and this usually means clarifying whose purposes are being served.

Much of the current effort in evaluating training and development, where it exists, is after the event and may well only consist of basic number crunching. It does not take into account the need to assess the training against objectives set well

11

in advance of the actual process and which are drawn from the institutional and departmental planning processes. In other words, all training and development should be in line with organisational and departmental objectives. A commitment to 'lifelong learning' or 'continuous professional development' features as an organisational objective in an increasing number of organisations both within and outside higher education. If this commitment proves to have substance, evaluation will then be the first process to take place.

The context

Higher education exists to:

- plan, undertake, support and disseminate research, scholarship and related activities;
- design, implement, support and evaluate learning and teaching;
- develop and review strategy, and lead, manage and administer systems and services in support of academic practice. (UCoSDA, 1996)

The relationship between institutional and sectoral requirements and expectations, and effective evaluation of staff development must therefore be made quite clear. Staff development should clearly focus on the agreed core business, and virtually everything staff development does must be in support of the core business. If the core business is teaching, learning and research, all activities and any calculation of their worth or value or benefit must evidently be based on this premiss. This does not mean programmes such as how to avoid stress, assertion training and the like should be abandoned. On the contrary, the institution may well have articulated a wish to keep staff and to keep them at the peak of their effectiveness. 'People maintenance' training and development actions are, therefore, a part of realising this aim.

'Staff development is a crucial link in an institution's enhancement of the quality of student learning' (Barnett, 1992). Research linking staff development and the student experience is surprisingly scarce and rarely conclusive, although several studies do make this link, such as Ramsden (1983). In addition, the introduction of national staff development and training quality kitemarks, such as Investors in People, have positively encouraged, even forced, the connection to be made (Taylor and Thackwray, 1995, 1996).

The importance of effectively evaluating the benefits of training and development in higher education was highlighted by the Universities' and Colleges' Staff Development Agency (UCoSDA) in 1994 with the publication of *Continuing Professional Development (CPD) of Staff in Higher Education (HE): Informing Strategic Thinking* (see Appendix 1). The report was compiled by a 'Task Force' with representation drawn from a wide variety of UK higher education institutions. It began with a look at the implications of change in higher education and is a useful scene setting vehicle.

An Evaluation of Training and Development in Higher Education group was convened by UCoSDA (Universities and Colleges Staff Development Agency) as a natural extension of this task force to examine current practice and, on the basis of this, to prepare a guide to some of the main evaluation instruments. The proposal to create such a group emanated from a national conference held in June 1996 to look at evaluation. Elements of the conference are described more fully in Chapter 12.

The key questions

There are a few key questions that need to be asked and answered – by staff developers and institutions in general – before anything is done. There are many versions of these questions. A particularly useful version produced by Nevo (*New Directions in Educational Development*, ed House E, 1986) is reproduced below:

- How is evaluation defined?
- What are the functions of evaluation?
- What are the objects of evaluation?
- What kinds of information should be collected regarding each object?
- What criteria should be used to judge the merit of an evaluation object?
- Who should be served by an evaluation?
- What is the process of doing an evaluation?
- What methods of enquiry should be used?
- Who should do the evaluation?
- By what standards should the evaluation be judged?

Some practical questions can be added to the list such as: how and when should the results be presented?

Having established the ground rules at the outset, issues can then be explored in a clear and focused way. Evaluation is the first element of the planning phase and not a bolt-on additional activity taking place after a training and development action, as such initiatives as Investors in People underline.

Evaluation is a systematic process with several component parts. It can vary considerably in form. Therefore evaluation can be empirical, statistical, illuminative and so on. It can produce qualitative and/or quantitative data.

Unless you know *why* you are evaluating – and for whom – the selection of the appropriate instruments is highly unlikely. Within higher education, the prevailing view is that training and development is not normally driven by institutional and departmental objectives. If this is the case, it follows that any evaluation of that training and development must be seriously flawed as it also must be set in the context of what the institution wishes to achieve. Failure to do so is likely to result in irrelevant data collection processes, the outcomes of which will not meet the interest of any group of stakeholders, be they students, assessors, auditors, staff or management.

Lessons from students

In the case of the students course and programme evaluation has for some considerable time rightly demanded that there should be some focus on students' educational experiences and their intellectual progression. (Barnett, 1992). Evaluation should take place throughout the course and continuous feedback should be sought. The results of this evaluation then inform and enhance teaching, learning and assessment practice and procedure for future students.

Clearly, higher education already has much in place with regard to evaluation of students' learning. These are transferable skills par excellence. They merely need to be seen as transferable (see Chapter 8). In order for this transfer to take place, strategies such as responsive evaluation, discussed in Chapter 4, and pay forward, discussed in Chapter 5, can be adapted along with appropriate evaluation instruments to help create an acceptable – and therefore probably more workable – system for higher education institutions.

Lessons for managers

The key players here are the staff with responsibility for people management. The sector needs to address and facilitate the development of effective methods to ensure that managers exercise their responsibility for:

- establishing and agreeing the objectives of training and development actions;
- actively seeking post-course feedback to confirm that development objectives have been met and arranging dissemination, or further development as appropriate;
- taking action to ensure that newly acquired skills and knowledge are being used in the work place.

There are, of course, pockets of good practice, several examples of which are captured in Chapter 12, but they are relatively few and far between and rarely consistent across a single institution. Also, where good practice exists at the local departmental level, management is often entirely unaware of it.

Chapter 4 on responsive evaluation encourages staff developers and other appropriate staff to seek and keep the involvement of all key stakeholders from the very earliest planning stages. This introductory section highlights some of the issues for consideration prior to embarking on such a journey. There are many strongly held views as to how far higher education institutions have moved towards becoming organisations in the business sense, and even stronger views as to whether this is a good idea anyway. Barnett (1991) notes that 'the modern university, subject to the claims, financial uncertainties and inspections visited on it by the wider society, is more of a corporation than its earlier counterparts'. Many imported management techniques have foundered in institutions where, as Bilham (1989) puts it, 'traditionally most academic staff have little concerned themselves with the university as the organisational form which made their professional activities possible. It was simply the backdrop'. I have noted in several institutions an antipathy amongst certain staff towards being regarded as part of the organisation or department, claiming that their 'team' comprises individuals working in the same field anywhere in the world!

Having said that staff developers and others should involve senior staff, consider at the outset how well those senior staff know their institution. What information do they currently look for and how do they get it? Is it management by anecdote or are there sophisticated reporting structures, and is staff development and evaluation a part of these structures? For what purpose is information, especially on training and development currently collected? Middlehurst (1993) describes seven 'cults' evidently relating to senior staff in higher education institutions. These are the cults of: the gifted amateur; heredity; deficiency; inadequacy; the implicit; selection; the intellectual. Whatever the 'cult' is in a particular institution or department, staff training and development has a clear role in asking questions such as 'what are the training and development implications?' about all decisions relating to managers' roles.

Managing the process

It is also necessary at the outset to investigate the management of the evaluation process. Decisions have to be made about a number of factors, including the appropriateness and validity of sampling if used; the means by which data will be collected in terms of time, frequency, place and anonymity; the means by which the data will be extracted – manually or electronically for example; who will process the data and select and apply the appropriate statistical instruments; and in what form the results will be conveyed (and to whom).

Chapter 12 offers some examples of current practice in higher education in this area. The UCoSDA Task Force mentioned earlier produced a list of twelve recommendations, included in full as part of Appendix 1. The recommendations point to the need for clearer strategic planning for continuous professional development for all staff; for there to be a clearer link between training and development activities, institutional objectives and external influences in a changing climate; more integration between the appraisal process and training and development; greater understanding of, and emphasis on, the role of departmental training and development activities; and a far greater use and understanding of the processes of evaluating the benefits of training and development. Finally, recommendation twelve states that: 'institutions and cross-institutional groupings and agencies should support action in all these areas, in order that HEIs may develop as "*learning organisations*", which will in turn enhance their own credibility as providers of and for learning.' What learning organisations actually are and what messages the concept may contain for higher education is discussed in the introduction to Section 3.

The CVCP's (Committee of Vice Chancellors and Principals) *Response to the National Committee of Inquiry into Higher Education* further underlines the need for 'universities and colleges of higher education to develop as learning organisations' (CVCP, 1996). Clearly, effective evaluation of training and development must be an integral part of that process.

In essence, higher education must evidently move away from seeing training and development as reactive and separate, and more towards a position where 'development' is no longer separate from 'management'.

Chapter 2

Kirkpatrick...

'What in me is dark illumine, what is low raise and support'

Milton, *Paradise Lost*

To answer the question 'What is evaluation?' a good starting point can be made with the Donald Kirkpatrick four-level model of evaluation. This chapter seeks to explore the model that, nearly four decades ago, revolutionised managers', trainers' and developers' thinking in this area. It is still without a doubt the main, and often only, approach of which most organisations are aware. Many trainers and developers will say unashamedly that they have yet to find something better or more appropriate. The longevity of acceptance of the model is noteworthy – Kirkpatrick's four-level model of evaluation was introduced via four articles in the *Journal for the American Society of Training Directors* between November 1958 and February 1959. (The journal is now called *Training and Development*.)

In essence, Kirkpatrick sought to stimulate those with responsibility for the management of training and development to increase their efforts in evaluating training and development actions. The model comprises four levels, or steps. It is important to note that many commentators use 'level' in this context as being indicative of superiority/inferiority. This is not necessarily the case and was not the intention of Kirkpatrick to establish a hierarchy of evaluation imperatives. Each level measures different but complementary aspects of a training and development action.

Reaction	what the participants felt about the project or programme – the 'happy sheet'
Learning	internal validation – were the objectives met?
Behaviour	external validation – has training transfer taken place?
Results	has the project/programme made a difference? ie, what has been the impact on the institution?

Figure 2.1: *Kirkpatrick's four-level model of evaluation*

Step 1: Reaction

Kirkpatrick defines this as 'how well trainees like a particular training programme. Evaluating in terms of reaction is the same as measuring trainees' feelings. **It does-n't measure any learning that takes place**' (author's emphasis). 'Like' can be interpreted as including such things as venue, catering, organisation and adminis-tration. All this information is clearly of potential value to those responsible for the delivery of that particular service, provided they receive relevant summary infor-mation in an appropriate and usable format.

Reaction is easy to measure and easier to quantify, therefore nearly all training and development managers employing some form of evaluation use it. Reaction has value and merit, but can very often be the only methodology employed. If this is the case, any results based only on this will be relatively meaningless, how-ever much the end product is dressed up by complex formulae and presentation styles.

The reaction sheet or 'happy sheet'

A good happy sheet knows what it wants, so the objectives of the exercise must be worked out in advance. It should not be treated as a 'one size fits all' exercise. Most higher education institutions spend time and effort looking for or developing a reusable model. There may well be core themes that apply to all, but the process must be bespoke to the activity, as is the case in several institutions described in Chapter 12. Kirkpatrick suggests that we:

- determine what we want to find out;
- use a written comment sheet with the items determined in the task above;
- design the sheet so that reactions can be tabulated and quantified;
- obtain honest reactions by making the sheet anonymous;
- allow participants to write additional comments not covered by the questions, designed to be tabulated and quantified.

Two points emerge in relation to anonymity. First, anonymity does not necessar-ily promote honesty, it may merely allow other irrelevant agendas to come into play. Second, there is the view that knowing who wrote what allows a clear and targeted response. This underlines the point about each evaluation being bespoke to the activity. Kirkpatrick was writing long before Optical Mark Reading (OMR) was widely available, but the technology makes the number crunching significantly easier and faster.

Determining how people *feel* about a programme has increased significance where staff development and training is not seen by senior staff as a central part of the management and development of the organisation. There are many instances of training and developmental programmes being abandoned, running into the sand or being subject to inappropriate criticism because they were not seen as important or relevant by certain senior staff. If this is the case, what were the programmes doing there anyway? Training and development actions should emerge as a result of the identification of institutional, departmental and individual needs. If that is how they actually *did* emerge, the importance and relevance *has* been established so critics are not conforming to agreed corporate policy and practice. Kirkpatrick asserts that people must *like* a training programme to 'obtain the most benefit', and quotes a former president of ASTD 'It's not enough to say, "Here's the information, take it". We must make it interesting and motivate people to want to take it'.

Staff developers should make their own appraisal of the training in order to supplement participants' reactions. The combination of two such evaluations is more meaningful than either one by itself. An example of self-appraisal in practice at the University of Newcastle is described in Chapter 12. Again, Kirkpatrick notes that although the results of this exercise may show whether the activity 'went well', there is no evidence that learning has taken place, that participants' working practice will be improved and that this improvement can be attributed to the training activity.

Step 2: Learning

The analysis of reactions enables the staff developer to determine how well a programme or event was received. In addition, comments and suggestions will be obtained that will be helpful in enhancing the quality of future training and development actions and the various other services that support the process, such as catering and administration.

Although it's important to get a positive response, favourable reactions 'don't assure learning'. Decisions on level, type and nature of future training and development actions and the resourcing of these actions are, in higher education, often based on the reactions of one or more key people.

We evidently do tend to pay more attention if the presenter is witty, stylish, well prepared and uses state-of-the-art technology. However, if content is analysed it may show that nothing of any real value was actually said! Therefore, argues Kirkpatrick, it's important to determine objectively the amount of learning that actually takes place. Kirkpatrick uses a somewhat limited definition of learning here, ie what principles, facts, and techniques were understood and absorbed by trainees? He offers the following 'guideposts' for measuring learning:

- Measure the learning of each trainee so that quantitative results can be determined.
- Use a before-and-after approach so that learning can be related to the programme.
- As much as possible, the learning should be measured on an objective basis.
- Where possible, use a control group (not receiving the training) to compare with the experimental group that receives the training.
- Where possible, analyse the evaluation results statistically so that learning can be proven in terms of correlation or level of confidence.

Clearly, the evaluation of learning is more difficult than the evaluation of reaction. Like many later writers, Kirkpatrick argues that a knowledge of statistics is necessary, although, interestingly, does not necessarily believe that this should be done by a staff development and training unit or equivalent. 'In many cases, the training department will have to call on a statistician to plan the evaluation procedures, analyse the data, and interpret the results'. Organisations operating under a transfer pricing system (see Chapter 5) often have the evaluation function completely separate, in terms of staffing, from the training and development function.

Kirkpatrick notes that 'it's relatively easy to measure learning that takes place in training on skills'. Evaluation of learning is incorporated into the process by setting up 'before-and-after situations in which trainees demonstrate whether they know the principles or techniques being taught'. In other words, clear criteria are set with regard to the expected outcomes. Taylor and Thackwray (1997) produced a simple log-book format as a basis for agreeing objectives and evaluating learning and the application of that learning (see Appendix 2).

Kirkpatrick recommends the use of testing when principles and facts rather than techniques are taught. He also counsels *against* the use of pre-prepared standardised tests and *for* the use of 'bespoke' material, on the grounds that the external package will only be able to contribute to part of the overall evaluation.

As an argument for securing departmental and institutional support, proving the effectiveness of training and development actions in terms of learning as well as reaction, evaluation of *learning* is demonstrably more powerful than reaction in isolation.

Step 3: Behaviour

Kirkpatrick (1959) tells this story:

'When I joined the Management Institute of the University of Wisconsin in 1949, one of my first assignments was to observe a one-week course on human relations for foremen and supervisors. I was particularly impressed by Herman, a foreman from a Milwaukee company. Whenever the instructor asked a question about human relations, Herman raised his hand. He had all the answers. I thought, "If I were in industry, I'd like to work for someone like Herman." It so happened that my cousin, Jim, worked at Herman's company and Herman was his boss. Jim told me that Herman may know all about the principles of human relations but he didn't practice them on the job. He performed as a typical "bull-of-the-woods" who had little consideration for subordinates' feelings and ideas. I realised that there was a big difference between knowing principles and techniques and using them on the job.'

In an environment such as higher education where a substantial element of the workforce is highly articulate and educated to at least first degree level, it would be naive to assume that a significant number of senior managers did not know the 'principles of human relations'. Indeed, many staff at a variety of levels have commented negatively on the growth of 'quickie' management qualifications ('Instant MBAs – just add hot air!'; 'Management By Amateurs.') However, experience suggests that, as with Herman above, *knowing* does not necessarily correlate with *doing*. The 'gap' is often between the real and stated rationale as to why the training is taking place; the ever present struggle between rhetoric and reality. Becher (1989) identifies four categories of university organisation; hierarchical, collegial, anarchical and political. Pluralistic values and ambiguous goals are features of one type; conflict being the basis for decisions is a feature of another. The staff developer and staff with responsibility for people management need to be very aware of the culture of their institution, and to be able to *act on this knowledge*. (All four of Becher's categories are described more fully in Chapter 4.)

Some years ago a former colleague was invited by a Vice Chancellor of a new university to put together a short event for senior and middle managers on issues of equality of opportunity, because all staff should know about it – 'we're an equal opportunities organisation'. An unusual phrase introduced the Vice Chancellor's actual rationale: 'I have a rose garden here and it has greenfly. I want you to provide a spray'. Beneath the publicly stated rationale – to continue to strive towards equality of opportunity, to widen participation and so on – lay the real reason. There were too many inappropriate activities relating to recruitment and selection practices. These were costing money and creating bad publicity. Real evaluation of this event, therefore, would have compared the range, number and level of complaints, law suits, tribunals, etc before and after the event. However, like much training and development of its kind, the real reasons were never articulated in the public domain, with the result that real evaluation was impossible. A different and irrelevant answer has been given to the first key question – why are you doing it?

Kirkpatrick offers the following criteria of desirable characteristics of individuals engaging on a development activity.

- *They must want to improve.* Is the reason for undertaking research to do with the individual's interest, or in the interest of the research assessment exercise, or a combination of both?

- *They must recognise their own weaknesses*. This is difficult. Many higher education institutions reported considerable paranoia when observation of teaching was first introduced. Also the word *'weakness'* I feel, is not used appropriately in this context – the focus should be on, and in the spirit of, continuous improvement.
- *They must work in a permissive climate*. Arguably this is the case for almost half the staff in higher education. Many would, on the other hand, argue that academic freedom and integrity has been significantly eroded over the past few years. The message for senior managers is to encourage and support measures that promote autonomy and academic integrity. See Chapter 10 on the University of East London's Quality Improvement in Learning and Teaching (QILT) project evaluation.
- *They must have help from someone who is interested and skilled*.
- *They must have an opportunity to try out new ideas*.

These last two criteria sit well with what many imagine higher education to be. The reality, for certain categories of employee, such as those working in various support roles, can be very different. Examples include differential access to, and support for, undertaking research, and permission actually to participate in some development activities.

Evaluation of the result of training and development actions in terms of behaviour back at work is more difficult than reaction and learning evaluations. It requires a more scientific approach and the consideration of a range of factors. Again, Kirkpatrick offers 'guideposts', this time for evaluating training in terms of behavioural changes.

- appraise performance before and after the development action has taken place;
- have the appraisal conducted by peers, staff developers, departmental heads or any other colleague familiar with the individual's professional development (the more the better);
- statistically analyse the results to compare before-and-after performance and to relate such changes to the training and development actions;
- have a post-training appraisal three months or more after the training action so that participants have an opportunity to put into practice what they learned. Subsequent appraisals may add to validity of the study;
- use a control group.

Employee attitude surveys before and after training and development actions may be of use here (see Chapter 6). Material produced in support of achieving Investors in People status could be used – there are managers' and employees' surveys that can, and have been, easily adapted to higher education (see Chapter 7). The least evaluated form of training within higher education is management training, which paradoxically accounts for the biggest spending by a considerable margin. The Industrial Society's survey of all sectors shows management development to be the *most evaluated* form in other sectors (see Chapter 11). This discrepancy can be in part accounted for by an evident reluctance of many senior managers in higher education to subject themselves to internal scrutiny and review of any sort. To evaluate the impact of their own professional development activities it is necessary to get the reflections of both peers and subordinates with regard to observed changes in professional practice. Upward appraisal and 360° appraisal are not much in evidence in higher education.

Step 4: Results

Results is the most difficult area to evaluate effectively and this was recognised by Kirkpatrick. Although the objectives of most training and development actions can be stated in terms of outcomes, 'complicating factors can make it difficult, if not impossible, to evaluate certain kinds of programmes in terms of results' (Kirkpatrick, 1959).

Instructional training, such as some elements of IT programmes lend themselves quite easily to a 'before and after' approach. It is easy to suggest that this is also true for more complex forms of development such as preparing to publish. For example, if an institutional priority was to increase the number of publications, there are several ways in which this could be addressed. A training and development programme targeting neophytes could be arranged, as could a mentoring scheme utilising the skills of senior staff with an excellent track record in publishing. The before and after evaluation would simply count the number of publications. This falls into the trap of monocausality and becomes a hostage to fortune. An improved level of publication could relate to changes in the number of opportunities to publish (more journals), changes in the pressure to publish (research assessment exercise approaching), a new breakthrough in the area of study and so on. In other words, there are so many variables it is difficult to separate them. It would be far easier – and more meaningful – to evaluate results in terms of the contribution made by training and development actions by using peer and self-assessment. Kirkpatrick advocated a participative approach to this level, noting that where it was applied it resulted in 'better feelings, attitudes, and other human relations factors'. He also predicted that there would be growing interest in this level in the future, although his hope was to be able to 'measure human relations training in terms of dollars'. It would be more appropriate to measure results in terms of an institution's capacity to learn, change and develop in line with its agreed objectives.

The effectiveness of staff developers and the training and development activities that fall within their remit is obviously the key measure. However, to determine effectiveness, outcomes of training and development actions must be measured. The skills for this do not necessarily reside within staff development units, so consideration needs to be given to the development of the developers, or bringing in outside expertise, as many proponents of transfer pricing would argue.

Chapter 3

... and After

'We trained very hard, but it seemed that every time we were beginning to form up in teams, we would be reorganised. I was to learn later in life that we tend to meet any new situation by reorganising, and a wonderful method it can be for creating the illusion of progress, whilst producing confusion, inefficiency and demoralisation.'

Caius Petronius (AD 66)

There are, of course, critics of Kirkpatrick. Although it is rather redolent of the story of the emperors clothes for anyone in higher education to repeat them, there may be some useful hints on planning and delivering a comprehensive evaluation strategy that suits higher education and is 'bespoke' to a particular institution or department. Here's a slightly modified version of Kirkpatrick's four-level evaluation model, adapted to include measuring for return on investment.

Level	Questions
Reaction and planned action	What are participant reactions to the training? What do they plan to do with the material?
Learning	What skills, knowledge, or attitudes have changed? By how much?
On-the-job application	Did participants apply on the job what they learned in training?
Business results	Did the on-the-job applications produce measurable results?
Return on investment	Did the monetary value of the results exceed the cost of training and/or development action?

Figure 3.1: *Kirkpatrick's four-level evaluation model, adapted to include measuring for return on investment*

The Context, Input, Reaction and Outcome (CIRO) Approach

A broad approach to classifying evaluation was taken by Warr, Bird and Rackham (1970). The four areas, Context, Input, Reaction and Outcome evaluation can be summarised as follows:

- *Context evaluation* involves deciding whether there is a need for any action, basing that decision on management information. Objectives are agreed in three categories: the ultimate objective and two intermediate objectives relating to changes in behaviour and acquisition of new skills.
- *Input evaluation* basically decides on the best method of delivery, taking into account such factors as mode, timing and style of delivery, level and type involvement of staff, financial factors.
- *Reaction evaluation* is, as it suggests, used to determine participants' reactions based on individual reports or interviews.
- *Outcome evaluation* uses the results to inform future planning, notably with regard to the formulation of general and specific objectives and the setting of criteria by which success will be measured.

Critics of Kirkpatrick assert that the four-level training evaluation process may not always produce genuinely meaningful, long-term results. Consequently, planning with regard to evaluation may operate within inappropriately limited parameters. The result is a reduction in the institution's ability to conduct relevant and useful evaluations.

Kirkpatrick's model implies that conducting an evaluation is a standardised, pre-packaged process. This clearly is not always the case, nor is it desirable to present evaluation as something that produces facts, as opposed to management information on achievement or otherwise of institutional targets. There is a range of issues raised by this. Several of these issues can be categorised as myths. Here are some myths about evaluation.

Myth	Comment
An evaluation is definitive	Most evaluation activity appears to believe in monocausality. In other words, a single evaluation action can be used to answer all questions (one size fits all, again). This approach is not prepared for ambiguous findings. Nor is much attention paid to the impact of varying levels of methodological rigour. Credibility and accuracy are not established and maintained by one type of evaluation.
To evaluate is to be effective	Questions must be asked and an agenda agreed before any action is taken. Why is the evaluation taking place? Who wants it? Why do they want it? What are they planning to do with the information? (See Chapter 4.)
Staff developers are responsible and/or accountable for effectiveness	Greater attention should be given to clarifying exactly what the staff development and training department is responsible for and is thereforeaccountable for. Clear criteria should be agreed at the outset as to what comprises effectiveness. Being held accountable for quality of content, for example, may or may not be appropriate. The people best placed to support and assess the transfer of learning are those staff with people management responsibilities. The role of staff development is to support this process.
Kirkpatrick's level four, impact on the organisation, is the most important	This is certainly where the gaps are in higher education. I do not see any level necessarily having 'superiority' over another. Although there are clear links, they measure different things. Measures employed for one level are not necessarily transferable to another.
Quantification is essential	Quantification is not essential. However, agreement on what the institution hopes to get out of the activity and how this will be measured is essential. In other words, success criteria can be both quantitative and qualitative, but these criteria must be agreed by all stakeholders in advance.

Figure 3.2: *Some myths about evaluation*

)ers and trainers should not employ the model without assessing needs
y for higher education at the moment, resources. Actual application of
an also be a neglected area. Critics suggest that when the Kirkpatrick
model is used as a universal framework for all evaluations, it can be the *model itself*
that is shaping the process and, therefore, the results.

Bernthal's approach

Bernthal (1995) identifies seven steps in the setting up of a 'long-distance', in-depth
evaluation programme.

Bernthal's Seven Steps

Step 1: Identify the organisation's values and practices.
Step 2: Identify skills, knowledge, and attitudes.
Step 3: Define the scope and purpose of the evaluation.
Step 4: Identify data sources.
Step 5: Choose the best method for collecting data.
Step 6: Select the best measurement approach.
Step 7: Gather and inventory your resources.

Figure 3.3: *Bernthal's seven steps*

Step 1: Identify the organisation's values and practices

Most universities and colleges have mission or vision statements. These statements
are not always perceived to be put into practice. In identifying a higher education
institution's *actual* core values it is necessary to link them to *actual* practices. If, for
example, one of the stated values is 'teamwork', does it occur in reality? If so, are
individual objectives linked to departmental objectives, and are those departmental
objectives linked back to a declared institutional value of teamwork?

Step 2: Identify skills, knowledge, and attitudes

Having made the link between policy and practice, it is then easier to identify the
type of activity that will enable staff to improve performance in such a climate. To
facilitate this, production of a list of skills and knowledge requirements linked to
the identified practices can be undertaken.

If analysis of training and development needs is not a regular feature of the institution, then the following will need to be taken into consideration. Training Needs
Analysis (TNA) is sometimes seen as a logical starting point for the evaluation

process in tandem with strategic planning. TNA is the term used by most other sectors. Much of higher education has a problem with the language. It may be more appropriate to convert this and other jargonistic terminology into acceptable *lingua franca* for colleagues as appropriate, such as Staff Development Analysis or Professional Development Analysis. Either way, the TNA should seek to identify the following:

- the knowledge and skills the training or development action needs to address;
- a profile of the target audience in terms of learning experiences and preferences, attitudes, range of existing knowledge and skills, personal attributes, previous work-based experience and so on;
- non-training/non-development issues which may impact upon performance;
- training/development related issues which may impact on the mastery of objectives and on the transfer of learned skills/knowledge into practice.

Step 3: Define the scope and purpose of the evaluation

Having established how training and development 'fits' within an organisation, a series of questions can be generated. Effective evaluation should, it is argued, measure more than the Kirkpatrick levels of reaction, learning, behaviour, and results. Those levels focus primarily on outcomes and do not take into account *processes* leading to the results.

There are several areas beyond Kirkpatrick's four levels that can be evaluated. These include:

- the quality, delivery, and/or retention of the training and development action;
- whether the training and development action solved a problem or an issue for a particular group of staff;
- how useful 'parallel' training and development is for managers and their staff (eg, appraisal – appraiser and 'appraisee');
- variables in the work environment that discourage or facilitate the effect of training and development actions;
- organisational context. There are barriers that hinder and factors that encourage and support the training and development effort.

A useful exercise is to list the barriers to training and development and those factors that encourage, support and enhance training and development, and then to set these alongside the potential outcomes of pursuing this route. Focus groups or similar drawn from identified key stakeholders can be used in support of this process.

Step 4: Identify data sources

The quality of evaluation data depends on the source. For example, self-assessment may not be the best way to determine whether a person's behaviour has actually changed as a result of a training or development action. Criteria for choosing the best sources of data include objectivity, accessibility, and reliability. Sources should be:

- unbiased;
- able to provide understandable information;
- easy to access; and
- able to produce uncontaminated information.

Ideally, therefore, information should have 'validity, reliability and practicality' (Newble and Cannon, 1991).

Step 5: Choose the best method for collecting data

Any *appropriate* research methodology can be employed. The emphasis on appropriateness relates to Juran's fitness for purpose and practical limitations.

Step 6: Select the best measurement approach

If the methods employed to evaluate a training and development action are simplistic, or if only one method is employed, the result will not be objective and subject to critical review, justified and/or unjustified, thus devaluing any impact it may have. Therefore, to increase objectivity, a variety of methods and approaches should be employed.

Step 7: Gather and inventory your resources

The final stage is to identify the people who will assist in the evaluative process. What are their skills? Which parts of the process should they be responsible for? Do they have enough power and influence in the institution or department to act on and implement salient outcomes?

The 'Endless Belt' of Development

The UK Industrial Society recommends this method of evaluation. It incorporates validation and encourages a cyclical approach as follows:

- defining objectives that relate to business needs;
- designing an appropriate learning process;
- assessing the performance of participants before and after the learning process;
- measuring the lasting benefits for the individual and for the organisation.

(The Industrial Society Survey, 1994)

The Endless Belt comprises six stages as shown below. Devotees claim that it does not clash with other approaches, such as Kirkpatrick, and that it is better because 'it starts earlier'.

The Endless Belt of Development		
Stage	**Activity**	**Comments**
Stage 1	Recognise a business need	This might be a particular target, such as improving research assessment ratings, or dealing with a problem such as levels of complaints, or launching a new activity or a reorganisation. A business need does not always generate a training and development action.
Stage 2	Define development objectives	This should be done via appropriate consultation and discussion with stakeholders, the key players being the line manager and the provider/facilitator of the action.
Stage 3	Design learning process	An appropriate route is agreed – perhaps offsite and classroom based, assigning a mentor, a short secondment, or an NVQ. Wherever possible ensure the method is 'bespoke' to the learner. (See Chapter 8.)
Stage 4	Experience learning process	Typically, the participant will be given several opportunities to reflect and absorb, possibly including the recording of views in a reflective journal or training log. Reaction sheets and questionnaires will also be used. The reaction sheet will validate the event by checking that what was intended to be covered was covered, and the questionnaire will measure learning before application. (A test can also be used but may be inappropriate to many forms of development in higher education.)
Stage 5	Use and reinforce learning	In essence this is the key to embedding the new learning into working practices. The line manager

		is the key player here and will agree actions to ensure embedding.
Stage 6	Judge benefit to the organisation	At least several months after the completion of the training and development action, the impact on the organisation should be assessed. This should be done by comparing stages 2 and 5, ie the link between development objectives and operationalisation. Outcomes, including examples of return on investment if appropriate, are fed back into stage 1, and the 'endless belt' continues.

Figure 3.4: *The Endless Belt of Development*

An example of a simple form that records agreed objectives, relates them to the work objectives, agrees criteria, identifies what support is needed and reviews the action in both the long and short term can be found in Appendix 2.

The Institute of Personnel Development (IPD) is producing what might be seen as a developed version of the Endless Belt in the form of a toolkit. At the time of writing it is in draft form. It divides into two sections. In the first section, an overview of the organisational benefits of investing in learning is set out. The second section 'works through a model of the process of investing in learning and evaluating the impact of that investment'. It is doubtful whether the style and, indeed, elements of the various methodologies would suit many institutions in higher education. To some extent, however, it does help underpin the pay forward model described in Chapter 5, especially with regard to the involvement of senior management. The IPD uses Kirkpatricks' four levels, but includes material on establishing parameters, setting the learning objectives and measuring the return on investment. Level four is 'Evaluating the Impact on Business Performance' and includes guidance on the following methods, some of which are discussed in Chapter 5:

- structured interviews with senior management;
- senior management estimate of benefits;
- trend line analysis;
- impact analysis;
- organisational elements model;
- control group and pilots;
- management information.

In essence, we have come full circle. Those criticisms levelled at Kirkpatrick described earlier in this chapter could also be applied here (especially the myths). That would not be constructive. If all organisations in the UK at least followed Kirkpatrick, billions of pounds would be saved every year. The 1994 IPD survey of 467 companies showed that almost a fifth carried out no systematic evaluation of training. Eighty per cent of the ones that did employ some form of evaluation used reaction sheets, dropping to only 14 per cent who had a follow-up line manager questionnaire a few months later (see Chapter 11).

For the higher education sector, the most relevant, and therefore productive, way forward may lie in a broader and more flexible approach that incorporates the best of pay forward (see Chapter 5) and responsive evaluation (see Chapter 4).

Chapter 4

Responsive Evaluation

'Nid da lle gellir gwell' (It is not good if it could be better)

Welsh proverb

The goal-based evaluation methods of Kirkpatrick and others such as Warr, Bird and Rackham have fallen out of favour somewhat over the past twenty years. This is largely due to the growth in awareness, interest and understanding with regard to the highly political nature of evaluation and the selection and use of evaluation strategies. The assessment of the quality of university and college provision is often based on peer review. These peers are stakeholders. A narrow definition of responsive evaluation would be limited to finding out the views of stakeholders and presenting them in a usable format. A broader definition, and the one that applies to this book, includes the whole range of types of evaluation set in the context of what the institution wants/needs combined with the best methods of meeting these wants/needs. Therefore, responsive evaluation can make use of any strategy, having first secured agreement on purpose and function (ie, intended use by intended users). Some examples of evaluation 'types' are shown below (for further examples, especially financial measures, see Chapter 5).

Type	Example
Compliance	legal, sectoral or institutional requirements
Criterion focused	quality, stakeholder satisfaction
Developmental	the staff developer (evaluator) is part of the group that designs/develops/delivers the training or development action
External	independent specialists are used, often to enhance credibility
Goal based	Research assessment exercise performance
Longitudinal	a study of participants and training and development actions over a period of time – has investment in programmes supporting research and research-related activities resulted in enhanced Research Assessment Exercise performance?
Norm referenced	performance comparison with subject areas in other institutions
Participatory	direct involvement of participants, as in a review of peer observation of teaching by the group itself
Process	day-to-day operational issues and improvement of services in support of the delivery of training and development actions
Quality assurance	are minimum and accepted standards being routinely and systematically provided?

Figure 4.1: *Types of evaluation*

Stake (1975) coined the phrase 'responsive evaluation' and argues that evaluation should be concerned more with the interests of the various stakeholders (his three types of stakeholder are, *agents, beneficiaries and victims*). The interests of the stakeholders are divided into *claims, concerns* and *issues*. The first task for the evaluator, therefore, is to identify who the stakeholders actually are.

Legge (1984), writing on the evaluation of planned organisational change, notes that in addition to most research in this area being badly designed, rigorous evaluation research is so limited in scope as to be of little value to anyone. Rather than attempt such obviously flawed practice, a contingent approach should be adopted, asking questions relating to purpose and methodology. Bramley (1996) summarises these as four key questions, and I have modified them to broaden their scope as follows:

- Do you want the proposed training and development action to be evaluated?
- What functions do you wish the evaluation to serve?
- Which approach (list alternatives) best suits the requirements of the activity?
- To what extent are constraints resulting from this approach acceptable?

Responsive evaluation may be more attractive to higher education, given that it offers the opportunity to discuss the meaning of truth, recognises that any evaluation will be a mixture of fact, and values and that it is normally not possible to generalise from an evaluation.

What is meant by responsive evaluation?

Current evaluation strategies emphasise quantitative data rather than qualitative data to demonstrate worth or value. Bluntly, the measures applied normally comprise 'bums on seats and number of courses'. The other popular measure is to monitor participant reaction to training and development actions, on a numerical scale, with the ubiquitous 'happy sheet' or reaction sheet.

With the exception of classroom-based instructional type training activities, justifying effectiveness of training and development actions appears to be one of a set of measures that apply a numerical/financial 'value' to the results of the activity. Typical financial methods, such as cost benefit analysis, return on investment and others are described in Chapter 5.

If these are the only measures employed, evaluation may well run into difficulties in higher education, insofar as it is very unlikely that it can be satisfactorily proven that a particular training programme or development action has actually caused any benefits claimed. Often, proof is impossible to find; too many other variables are in play and, of course, nothing is monocausal. However, linking training and development actions to individual, departmental and institutional outcomes is absolutely essential. The process of creating such a link is ambiguous and highly interpretative, especially in complex organisations like universities and colleges.

When evaluating training and development, the critical activity is the collection of evidence that suggests, and preferably demonstrates, a causal relationship between action and results. The creativity is in developing that link. A responsive evaluation strategy can be made to pay attention to both 'hard' and 'soft' issues. It does not minimise the importance of showing outcome-oriented results of training, but does recognise that perceptions about training and development are shaped by many qualitative factors.

Philips (1991) describes responsive evaluation as a 'both/and' approach, rather than an 'either/or' approach. It is both quantitative and qualitative; it is both summative and formative. It deals with process as well as outcome.

It is a really a question, again, of fitness for purpose. Sometimes quantitative, out-come-oriented information is more effective, and other times qualitative, process-oriented information is more effective. The key is paying attention to the political nature of the institution (see Becher's classification of higher education institutions later in this chapter) and using the appropriate measures at the right times. The responsive model has as its objective the transferring of information to stakehold-ers so that they can act on the results. In order to be useful, any information must be translated so that it is meaningful to the people who are being informed. Every-one will perceive and respond to information in a different way, therefore it is dif-ficult to assess in advance exactly what will be meaningful to them.

Stake argues that responsive evaluation recognises the personal and political aspects of decision making. If responsive evaluation is to be employed effectively, there are certain basic 'rules' that must be employed in order for it to be beneficial. These are:

- Know your organisation – and be known in it.
- Be especially well-informed with regard to those who allocate funding or con-tribute to the funding of staff development.
- Don't produce huge amounts of data.
- Incorporate the data into user-friendly material for stakeholders.
- In preparing material, keep in mind who will be using the information and for what purpose(s).

Who are the stakeholders?

Stakeholders should be identified at the earliest opportunity: who is involved and in what capacity from the outset? Who should be involved? Who thinks they ought to be involved and isn't? and so on. Ask three key questions of the stakeholders, whether self-styled or actual:

- Why is this training and development action important to them?
- What actually is their stake in it?
- What values, biases, or experiences might influence their judgement about the programme?

This element of the process should enable useful communication to take place between the staff developer and the stakeholders. (Adapted from Philips, 1991).

What are the stakeholders information needs?

Basically:

- what do they want to know;
- why do they want to know it; and
- what are they going to do with the information.

A simple example would be developmental activity in support of preparation for the Research Assessment Exercise. One way to get this information from stakeholders is to ask them for it by interview, at a staff development meeting, at Academic Board or equivalent, or via their own departmental/faculty meetings. If the various stakeholders can be brought together as a group this will also offer the advantage of starting to create a degree of uniformity and ownership of the activity. Philips also suggests we find out what questions the stakeholders themselves have. If they have no questions about a training and development action, they are unlikely to be interested in, or to use, any evaluative information in whatever form it is presented.

Some universities and colleges are so large that it's difficult to have direct access to stakeholders, and sometimes even to work out who they actually are. In such cases, the evaluation strategy is more political than personal. The principle is essentially the same – to identify the needs of the stakeholders. It helps if a sense of the key stakeholders' personal priorities, concerns, and preferred communication styles is developed. Higher education is going through a time of great change, so more than ever the staff developer needs to have direct access to at least one key decision maker. This direct access should enable greater awareness of political factors and the various inevitable 'hidden agendas'.

What data to use?

Collecting and using both quantitative and qualitative methods to evaluate training and development actions will improve the staff developer's ability to get actions implemented. The pay forward model, where development is no longer separate from management, is particularly useful here. Responsive evaluation can also measure quantitative elements of training and development actions.

Many senior managers in higher education prefer quantitative information because they believe that it represents hard, objective data, although this is not necessarily the case. There is also no reliable way to gather quantitative data on some important aspects of training or development. The end result is often a combination of guesswork and invention, and is therefore relatively meaningless. The number crunching should be made 'purposeful and thereby meaningful' as opposed to not doing it. Therefore, when the advantages and disadvantages of quantitative and qualitative data are known, the staff developer can encourage stakeholders to focus on the agreed important issues. Clearly, for instance, quantified data will give no indication of attitude change or a rise or fall in morale. It is absolutely necessary, therefore, to look at meaning:

- what does the training and development action *mean* to participants?
- what does it *mean* to the core business of the institution – teaching, learning, research?

Measurement of quality is often descriptive and comes in forms such as anecdotes, case studies or 'audit trails'. 'Indicators of Programme Quality' (HEQC, 1996) contains useful examples of both hard and soft measures (see Chapter 8).

Different methodologies are employed in the gathering of different types of data. In other sectors, as Philips (1991) points out, numerical data that are tied to business results are often monitored through such methods as 'surveys, productivity measures (such as the sales volume, the size of an average sale, or the number of incentive bonuses), and quality measures (such as reductions in error, waste, rework, or customer complaints)'. In higher education we should look, for example, to staff and student recruitment, retention and progression, or the number and value of research grants.

Qualitative data is gathered via such methods as interviews, focus groups, observations, or open-ended questionnaires. This allows for anecdotes, audit trails and so on to be collected in order to broaden the evaluation of specific training and development actions, such as examples of how new skills and/or knowledge are being applied (Kirkpatrick level three).

The obvious criticism of qualitative data is that it can be seen as subjective, but relying solely or too heavily on either type of data can easily result in inaccurate conclusions being drawn by stakeholders and the training and development function itself. Qualitative measures have made something of a comeback in the UK over recent years, not least because of the impact of the Investors in People initiative where audit trails, essentially triangulated anecdotes, are used as an effective means of assessing organisations against the National Standard.

Quantitative measures are equally subject to charges of misuse. Such measures can be outcome-oriented without providing any insight into the area of inquiry. Regardless of declared interest in statistical data, anecdotal material often holds more sway. Individual items of such information may not be seen to be of value. It is the synergy generated by constructively linking the results to form helpful and usable information for stakeholders that is of real and demonstrable value. Meaning can be enhanced by paying close attention to how the various parameters are set. The same information can be made to look very different depending on how it is made to 'stand out'. For senior staff, the information should be framed in terms of strategic objectives, but staff developers might also want to highlight certain other real concerns. Figure 4.2 illustrates one such concern in a somewhat over simplified way.

Indifference or hostility?	
Academic Subculture	**Management Subculture**
Importance of knowledge and understanding	Practical skills and outcomes
Focus on theory	Focus on practice
Emphasise cognitive skills	Emphasise action skills
Teach whatever they choose	Only teach practically relevant things
Research with the aim of publishing	Research with the aim of illuminating and solving problems
Consider personal success in terms of what is published and how important it is seen to be by peers only	Consider personal success in terms of the ability to define and address problems efficiently and effectively to the employer and the organisation's mission or profits

Figure 4.2: *From Murphy, J (1992) 'Quality university management programmes',* International Journal of Educational Management, *vol 6 no 2*

The key message here is to know your audience and to package information accordingly. Stakeholders should continue to be involved and informed throughout the planning cycle.

Philips uses a physics analogy to explain the difference between being responsive and being reactive: 'for every action there's an equal and opposite reaction. A mechanical reaction causes an object to be forcefully propelled in a particular direction, as with the propulsion of a jet engine'. Responsive evaluation of training and development also creates this via interactive dialogue with stakeholders. All feedback offered should therefore feed into the decisions behind the strategic management of the institution, providing the necessary clear link between development and management.

Feedback is not limited to verbal or written forms. There is increasing interest in electronic forms. E-mail, for example, as an interactive evaluative tool can be used at a variety of levels and in a variety of ways, as can institutions web pages or local intranet.

Decisions are the product of a variety of interrelated factors – opinion, fact, information, internal influence, external influence and so on – plus all of the personal 'baggage' brought to any decision-making process. Therefore, the best way to contribute to and influence a decision is to share information with stakeholders continuously.

Why bother?

A responsive evaluation strategy can help direct others' knowledge, perception and understanding of training and development. Focusing on the stakeholders, it links training and development to the wider goals and objectives of the institution. It is the job of the staff developer to provide enough evidence for that link to be established and for it to continue and strengthen. Therefore, who the stakeholders are and what they want to know must be clarified at the outset, and only then should the appropriate evaluation instruments be selected.

It is appropriate to reiterate that evaluation must be the first thing to be done. Criteria must be set prior to any training and development actions, and these actions must relate back to the departmental plan and thence to the institution's strategic plan.

What *should* be evaluated depends on what the purpose of the evaluation is. This will also impact on strategies and techniques used. Two useful examples of categories of evaluation follow.

Easterby–Smith (1994)	
Proving	Demonstrating something has happened because of training actions
Improving	Something becomes better than it currently is
Learning	Evaluation is an integral part of the development process
Control	Relating training actions to organisational objectives

Figure 4.3: *The Easterby–Smith categories of evaluation*

In essence, therefore, responsive evaluation asks the key question 'why should we evaluate?' We may wish to measure changes in attitudes, behaviour, skills knowledge or effectiveness. We may have other motives, some open, some less so. It is likely that there will be several, often competing, reasons for undertaking the evaluation of training and development. It is essential to 'know' your own institution in terms of how decisions actually get made. In other words, to be able to tease out the reality, not the rhetoric. Becher offers a useful classification of the political *modus operandi* for higher education institutions (see Figure 4.5).

Once you have worked out what sort of institution you belong to (it can easily be more than one of the above types at any one time, and can change from one to another over time and in different situations), then an appropriate strategy can be

Bramley (1996)	
Feedback evaluation	Provides 'quality control over the design and delivery of training activities'.
Control evaluation	Relates 'training policy and practice to organisational goals'.
Research evaluation	Seeks to 'add to knowledge of training and practice in a way which will have more general application than feedback evaluation'.
Intervention	
Power Games	

Figure 4.4: *The Bramley categories of evaluation*

worked out. The responsive model offers flexibility, depth and continuity, with staff developers contributing to the agenda of the organisation rather than being victims of it.

Any form of evaluation must have as its *raison d'être* the intention of being used as intended by the intended users. Anything else is a waste of resources.

Becher (1989)	
Hierarchical	In this system, authority is conferred from above. There are regulations, procedures, specified roles, and clear chains of command.
Collegial	The culture is a collegial one, with authority ratified from below and with decisions exposed to dissent. There is a high level of personal discretion.
Anarchical	Here, authority can be eroded by personal loyalties. Goals may be ambiguous and a pluralistic value system operates. The degree of influence of individuals and departments is based on expertise.
Political	Authority here derives from personal power. Conflict is seen as the main basis for decisions, the atmosphere is that of the politics of compromise with influence deriving from interest groups.

Figure 4.5: *Becher's classification of political* modus operandi

Section 2 Instruments and Strategies

Chapter 5

Some Instruments of Evaluation

'The Government ministries are very keen on amassing statistics. They collect them, raise them to the nth power, take the cube root, and prepare wonderful diagrams. But you must never forget that every one of these figures comes in the first place from the village watchman, who just puts down what he damn well pleases.'

Sir Josiah Stamp, economist, 1911

'VALIDITY – does it measure what it is supposed to?

RELIABILITY – are the results produced consistent and replicable?

PRACTICALITY– is it practical in terms of time and resources?'

Newble and Cannon, 1991

Most senior managers are now requesting information expressed in financial terms, and this trend is clearly set to continue. The theme throughout this book is that higher education does not do things less *effectively* than other sectors, just differently. There is no reason to import artificial and unworkable measures into the sector provided it can account for itself in a recognisable manner. At the moment there is little action in this area and no agreement as to what best might comprise a model for higher education. This chapter offers a summary account of some of the main financial methods, the previous chapter having set the scene for consideration of the appropriateness of any of these measures in a higher education context. In addition it focuses on transfer pricing, a system that has been the subject of some attention and scrutiny in a number of higher education institutions recently. Finally it looks briefly at various other instruments of evaluation.

Higher education is a sector of considerable substance, employing between 200,000 and 250,000 people (depending on who, when and why you ask), and with a total income of about £10 billion. Indeed, several individual institutions exceed £200 million in their own right.

Where financial instruments are used it is strongly recommended that there is an appropriate level of understanding of the sources of income and funding method-ologies for the sector, the institution and the department. There follows a very broad summary of some higher education funding sources and the methodology used in the allocation of these funds.

Sources of funding

There are two main sources – public and private. About two-thirds of higher education funding comes from public sources, mainly from central government, albeit via a series of convoluted routes. The most important route is via the higher education funding councils, each of which has its own method for allocating funds to individual institutions. Private sector sources include research grants, contracts and international students fees. Although currently accounting for a third of total income to the sector, private sector resourcing is increasingly important.

The largest single source of income to institutions is usually the block grant from the funding council. Teaching and research are the criteria that determine the level of the grant. For the teaching allocation, the following formula is applied to each subject category:

number of students x price per student = teaching based allocation

The research allocation is calculated on the basis of grades awarded in the Research Assessment Exercise as follows:

volume x price x quality multiplier = research based allocation

Financial instruments

Cost/benefit analysis

This is the most frequently used of the financial measures. It is simply a comparison of all the costs of a training and development action against all the benefits. (It is important to note that many of these 'benefits' are estimated, so the securing of stakeholder agreement in advance is essential.) The calculation is:

Net benefit = total benefit − total costs

Return on Investment (ROI)

This term originates from accounting and usually refers to the pre-tax contribution measured against controllable assets. In terms of evaluation, ROI moves cost benefit analysis up a gear. The calculation is:

ROI = [(benefits − costs) divided by costs] x 100

ROI is arguably of limited potential benefit to the evaluation of training and development in higher education. It's chief contribution may lie in demonstrating the value of specific activities such as induction, or local efficiency gains following purchase of new equipment (eg software).

Payback

Put simply, this looks at how long it will be before the total benefits of training and development actions exceed the total costs. The calculation is:

Payback period = total investment divided by annual savings

Profitability

Profitability is basically net income, ie what is left over after every possible item of expenditure has been taken into account. Often, the single biggest spend is on staff costs. This is evidently the case in higher education. Evaluating productivity using this single largest factor in expenditure can be done in a number of ways, including:

$$\text{Profits per employee} = \frac{\text{Trading profits}}{\text{Number of employees}}$$

$$\text{Output per employee} = \frac{\text{Units produced or processed}}{\text{Number of employees}}$$

$$\text{Value added per employee} = \frac{\text{Value added (sales revenue} - \text{cost of sales)}}{\text{Number of employees}}$$

Higher education being, apparently, a collection of not-for-profit organisations we should not be looking at net income as the 'bottom line', rather at budget surplus or, more typically, budget deficit. Naturally, to claim that certain training and development actions are solely responsible for particular financial improvements is courageous to say the least. Nevertheless, questions relating to the financing of staff development are increasingly being asked, and staff developers will need to be ready with answers.

Utility analysis

Utility is a function of the duration of a programme's effect on employees, the number of people trained, the validity of the training programme, the value of the activity for which the training was provided and the total cost of the programme (Philips, 1991). The formula for calculating this is:

$$\Delta U = T \, N \, dt \, Sdy - N \, C$$

Where:

ΔU = monetary value of the development activity

T = Duration and number of years of a development activity's impact on performance

N = Number of employees trained/developed

dt = True difference in job performance between the average trained/developed employees and the average untrained/developed employees in units of standard deviation

Sdy = Standard deviation of performance of the untrained/developed group in monetary terms

C = Cost of training/development per employee

It is hard to see how this and similar formulae could be of any real value to a higher education institution. There are too many variables, and defining such variables as the 'dt' element is unrealistic except in a very limited number of cases.

Transfer pricing

Techniques such as transfer pricing are used (rarely within higher education) to define and monitor the investment in staff development and training. It is appropriate here to examine this in some detail as a potentially useful strategy, demonstrating to all the real cost and value of staff training and development, and ensuring that anecdotes and assumptions do not excessively inform management thinking. (For example, there are many instances where senior staff assume that the employment of a trainer/staff developer means that that is exactly how they spend all their time – standing up in front of a group!)

As the pressure on institutions to seek ways of doing more for less continues to increase, so the need to tie staff development more closely to institutional objectives becomes more important. The current mechanism of allocating a sum of money does not promote cost consciousness, as is clearly demonstrated, for instance, by the number of 'no-shows'.

Staff development and training is seen by many colleagues in most higher education institutions as a monopoly supplier and an overhead. It is clear, therefore, that there may be benefits from a system that increases the local sense of ownership (and therefore participation), and at the same time addresses institutional issues and clearly demonstrates value for money. Transfer pricing is worth examining in this context.

What is transfer pricing?

Transfer pricing is the pricing of services delivered by the training and development function and the charging of faculties and departments for the services they have received. In effect, the central spend is on training and development that is either a legal requirement (eg health and safety) or an institutional requirement (eg corporate and local induction, induction for new teaching staff, appraisal etc). Other programmes are agreed with the appropriate unit and costs are clearly identified at the outset.

How is it implemented?

The first stage is initial costing. It is necessary to put a cost to *everything* relating to the delivery of training, including such activities as networking, advice, guidance and *ad hoc* discussions with colleagues that form the currently unquantifiable but essential soft benefit areas of staff development and training. For the *totality* of a training or development action, what is the cost of:

- staff
- accommodation
- overheads
- materials
- equipment
- external consultants/trainers

The cost is calculated via the establishing of systems within the training and development function to track time spent. The result should be that departments understand the costs and, in understanding the costs, the need to justify provision by the soft benefits argument decreases dramatically. It is demonstrably clear that training and development is not a free commodity. There is the opportunity to give background information on the cost of services.

Start up

Once key costs are calculated the consultation process can begin. This should aim to:

- agree with faculties and departments what will be provided;
- clarify the costs of the activities;
- identify any options on flexibility, for instance if a department wanted a stress management programme it could be over one afternoon or take the form of a 24-hour residential. A review of peer support activities by a course team, with the objective of identifying and meeting further training and development needs, could be a one-day programme or a series of two-hour sessions spread over the academic year;

- establish any spend limits;
- establish reporting back systems.

How do we operate in a transfer pricing environment?

The process should be robust (supported by systems) and analytical. It should be able to cope with competition from outside the institution. Detailed monitoring is possible, with data broken down into, for example, courses, materials, consultancy, etc, monitored by department, individually and institutionally.

What are the benefits?

- Cost consciousness
- Data on the real cost of services
- Talking directly to faculties and departments
- Offering costed options (reflecting the differential, spending power and priorities of individual units)
- Feedback
- Facilitating clearer prioritisation of services by staff development and clearer prioritisation of training and development needs by faculties and departments

What are the long-term implications?

These include an increased likelihood of change in the size of the training and development function. Working relationships between the 'centre' and the faculties and departments should be enhanced. There would be separate funding of institutional initiatives and a concentration on short-term objectives. It would also be easier to identify inefficient providers of training and development and take appropriate action accordingly.

Is it right for higher education?

In its present form probably not. It does, however, present possibilities for developing and piloting a higher education 'bespoke' model that would take account of, and recognise the existence and difference of the culture of the higher education sector. There are compelling arguments for a move away from menu-driven corporate staff development towards a negotiated and agreed set of activities, especially in the form of projects reflecting and supporting the delivery of institutional objectives. This process should also seek to move away from seeing development and training as an event or a series of events and towards seeing it as a multi-faceted service (see Chapters 9 and 10).

There has always been a tension between that which is clearly 'owned' by subject-specific/professional or vocational oriented development providers and that which is 'owned' by generic programme providers. It is a futile and potentially destructive exercise to endeavour to tease them apart, rather than to look at the best format for providing cohesive and measurable support for all forms of continuing professional development.

In summary, centrally driven programmes should include such clearly generic components as legally required, institutionally required and sectorally required activities. In addition some 'maintenance' type programmes can be included, such as those relating to information technology, and cross disciplinary activities like training and development programmes for departmental heads.

If these activities were costed in advance as described above, institutions would meet the twin objectives of increasing ownership at the local level and demonstrating cost effectiveness. Presumably all development would therefore be in line with corporate and business unit planning. This would also be very much in line with the requirements relating to Investors in People status.

Some other instruments

Pay forward

Pay forward is largely a response to the purely financial return instruments outlined above. It describes the benefits from training and development actions in terms of the organisation's capacity to learn and change. Arguably this is a more appropriate model for higher education, which should not exist to make a profit. The benefits from pay forward cannot be expressed in financial terms. Benefits are in the form of cultural/behavioural change, increased staff identification with institutional objectives, observed changes in individual or team behaviour or other changes. The key is that investment in training is not made to produce an end in itself, but rather to improve the organisation's ability to learn and change. Hence the notion that the benefits are 'projected into the future and cannot be identified separately from the outcomes of the wider change process'. The ultimate goal is to enable purely financial systems to 'fade into insignificance, since the training process is no longer separate from the business of managing' (Lee, 1996).

Impact analysis

In essence, impact analysis focuses on the importance of involvement of all key stakeholders prior to the delivery of the actual training and development action as discussed in Chapter 4.

Having secured the involvement of all stakeholders, key objectives for the· activity should be discussed and agreed, along with some agreement as to the areas for impact for follow-up evaluation. Clearly there are advantages insofar as stakeholder commitment and ownership can be built up, and possible disadvantages in terms of the time needed from these stakeholders. All three of Stake's stakeholders (the agents, beneficiaries and victims) should be involved in the discussions. It is possible that some people will fall into more than one category. For example, a proposal regarding the development of a cross-institution team of staff with responsibility for training and development locally may make the staff developer an agent (she or he will be facilitating the exercise), a victim (extra work/extra time/extra draw on resources) and a beneficiary (ultimately the improvement of training and development across the institution).

The standard method is to use post-it notes or similar for people to write the two or three most important outcomes as they see it. The post-its are collected, displayed on a wall and divided into related groups or themes. The themes are discussed and stakeholders are then given points to allocate to the theme or themes they believe represent the most important learning objectives.

When this exercise was undertaken by a major international oil company, the stakeholder group began by trying to agree what the key aspect of their business actually was. To the surprise of many, it turned out to be the specific act of getting the petrol into the car!

The stakeholder group then discusses and makes suggestions for the evaluation strategy for each of the learning objectives and the concomitant impact on institutional development and/or performance.

Trend

This is a simple statistical tool that can be used to look at possible relationships between data. When used in the evaluation of training and development this process looks at current trends in institutional (or unit) performance, forecasts performance and assesses the impact of learning on those trends. In essence, data relating to training and development actions would cover a number of analysis periods, say one year, and be converted from tables into a graph. The line through the data is the trend line.

The KPTM Ten Stage Model

This model, developed by Kearns and Miller, is linear – in contrast to the recent trend towards a cyclical approach. The model, although expressed in language that some elements within higher education may find difficult, offers an excellent opportunity to define and focus the corporate evaluation process from a value added perspective.

As mentioned elsewhere in this book, there is no point in evaluating everything. The KPTM model underlines this by arguing that there is a set of minimum skills that an employee can be expected to have. These are placed in 'box one'. Those training and development activities that give 'added value' and/or 'market edge' are placed in 'box two'. Only the contents of box two are evaluated. The entire process comprises analysis, design, delivery and evaluation and is summarised opposite:

Stage	
1	Business needs
2	Analysis
3a	Design
3b	Design
4	Agree (back to 3b to amend as appropriate)
5	Delivery
6	Reaction
7	Learning
8	Transfer
9	Value Added
10	Feedback

Figure 5.1: *The Ten Stage Model*

Which method?

The list of methods, instruments and strategies could be continued almost *ad infinitum*, but the many hundreds of models and techniques in the main merely repeat – using different terminology – much of what has gone before. It is more useful, therefore, to close this chapter by summarising evaluation methods in a table, slightly modified, originally prepared by Patton (1997). As noted earlier, the 'scientific' method was originally dominant and most evaluation, if it took place at all, was of instructional type training using the Kirkpatrick four levels or similar. The faith many managers place in apparently complex formulae is further evidence of this former dominance. The theme of this book is neatly encapsulated in the phrase 'intended use for intended users' (see purpose/synthesis in Figure 5.2 overleaf).

	Scientific paradigm	'Alternative' paradigm	Synthesis – a paradigm of choices
Purpose	Summative	Formative	Intended use for intended users
Measurement	Quantitative data	Qualitative data	Appropriate, credible, useful data
Design	Experimental design	Naturalistic inquiry	Creative, practical, situationally responsive designs
Researcher stance	Objectivity	Subjectivity	Fairness and balance
Inquiry mode	Deduction	Induction	Either or both
Conceptualisation	Independent and dependent variables	Holistic interdependent system	Stakeholder questions and issues
Relationships	Distance, detachment	Closeness, involvement	Collaborative, consultative
Approach to study of change	Pre-post measures, time series, static portrayals at discrete points in time	Process oriented, evolving, capturing ongoing dynamism	Developmental, action oriented. What needs to be known to get from where you are to where you want to be?
Relationship to prior knowledge	Confirmatory, hypothesis testing	Exploratory, hypothesis generating	Either or both
Sampling	Random, probabilistic	Purposeful, key informants	Combinations, depending on what information is needed
Primary approach to variations	Quantitative differences on uniform, standardised variables	Qualitative differences, uniqueness	Flexible: focus on comparisons most relevant to intended users and evaluation questions
Analysis	Descriptive and inferential statistics	Case studies, content and pattern analysis	Answers to stakeholders' questions
Types of statements	Generalisations	Context bound	Extrapolations
Contribution to theory	Validating theoretical propositions from scientific literature	Grounded theory	Describing, exploring and testing stakeholders' and programme's theory of action
Goals	Truth, scientific acceptance	Understanding, perspective	Utility, relevance. Acceptance by intended users.

Figure 5.2: *Adapted from Patton, 1997*

Chapter 6

Attitude, Behaviour and Effectiveness

'The discipline of colleges and universities is in general contrived not for the benefit of the students, but for the interest of, or more properly speaking, for the ease of the masters.'

Adam Smith, Correspondence of Sir John Sinclair, 1831

It is important to underline the difference between attitude and behaviour. An attitude is a predisposition to behave in a particular way, and behaviour relates to the individual's view as to what comprises the correct action for that particular situation at that particular time. An academic member of staff may have a strong aversion to undertaking a particular piece of research, but continues nevertheless because of the financial implications, or because of pressure from managers concerned about research ratings. Effectiveness, defined in the introduction as providing a better service with the same resources (ie increased benefits), would relate to success in achieving the objective of a higher rating by using the same resources better.

With regard to training and development, the method invariably used is to measure immediate reaction by multiple choice questionnaire – the happy sheet. Do we assume that because someone likes something they have learned something? Unfortunately, as discussed earlier, it seems that we do, as the happy sheet is the most commonly used form of evaluation in all types of organisations (see Chapter 11). Indeed, there is little or no evidence to support the notion that *enjoying* a conference, or any other form of training and development action, means that learning has taken place or, more importantly, that it translates into better working practices. Additionally, as already mentioned an important function of the reaction sheet – providing feedback to services that support the training and development effort – is also often overlooked.

Is it important to find out whether people enjoyed themselves? It may well be, but there should be a clear rationale set out in advance as to why this is necessary and what the information gained is going to be used for. For example, there may be a wish to find out what *type* of programme appeals to what category of employee. Do academic staff *like* different styles of training and development from technical staff? What variations exist between the learning styles of engineers and social scientists? Are there lessons to be learned in catering for different groups (see Chapter 8). Such information may be gleaned from people's attitude to the programme or event. The danger is in treating these responses as though nothing else is impacting on the group.

David Lodge, in his novel *Therapy*, offers an interesting illustration of this. The main character, a script writer, is very concerned that the studio audience response to his sitcom had been very poor. Only later does he learn that the audience had largely been made up of people from a factory that is to close, and they have all just received their redundancy notices with their pay-packets. Clearly, monocausality can afflict evaluation. One example familiar to all staff developers is the timing of events. Results of enquiries will invariably show that about 50% of people feel themselves to be too busy to spare any time during the week and opt for weekend conferences, and the other 50% become apoplectic at the thought of having to go to a conference at a weekend. It will be the same with trying to build in leisure time for the longer residential programme. Roughly half the people will demand it if it isn't there, and if there is free time and the other half will tell you they are not there for a holiday.

Evaluating the one-day/two-day event at the end of the session is often a waste of time. People are anxious to go (some will have gone), some may be reluctant to offend, others will think it their duty to offend, some may not wish to speak at all. Besides by the end it is too late to make adjustments anyway. In essence it is the personalities of the participants that comes through in the main, rather than how good or bad or useful the actual event has been.

Attitudes

All these instruments and techniques should be approached with extreme caution. They can go badly wrong, especially where the participants are well qualified and articulate. It is essential to ensure that presenters are in possession of both knowledge and skills at an appropriately high level.

The attitude training process

The evaluation process divides up into five complementary parts as described below, using as an example a group of academic staff who are being introduced to peer observation and support.

1. What is wanted?
Here, there must be agreement as to what attitudes are sought and how they will lead to some form of individual, group or organisational improvement. Such attitudes will by definition be general. Resolving to feel less hostile to the notion of people other than the students being in the lecture theatre is one example.

2. Where are we now?
The group is invited to self-assess their current working practices. These are then

set against the 'ideal'. The group may have concerns about confidentiality. Some may view the development as a management ploy to root out the 'weaker' members, others may be enthusiastic but apprehensive, and still others may resent the intrusion of the event and its expected outcomes on their research activities.

3. Why do we want to get there?
Participants, rightly, have to be convinced that the desired attitudes are 'right'. Observation and feedback are useful professionally, are popular with assessors and auditors of all types, and the ultimate beneficiary is the student.

4. How do we get there?
Techniques and strategies including role play/group work/video packages/guest speakers/students views on teaching and learning can all be used effectively.

5. How do we know we've got there?
The behaviour of people at work reflects the 'new' attitude. People recognise the individual and team benefits, and the practice of observation takes root as part of the 'life' of the department. New staff are locally inducted into the system. The activity is not seen as a bolt-on management led activity.

The repertory grid

This involves finding out what people think about a particular skill or attribute and what comprises 'good practice'. The technique was developed by a psychologist, George Kelly, and was designed to elicit a respondent's view of a particular issue, item or situation. Respondents produce their own list of constructs (characteristics) on which they rate items, such as colleagues. The resulting construct and item grid can then be used to describe how the respondent sees the particular issue, item or situation. The repertory grid is normally done on a one-to-one basis but works very well in groups which is often more practical due to time constraints.

The example group for this technique is senior managers brought together for a session on equal opportunities. To begin with, it is necessary to find out what they mean by equal opportunities, so they are asked to think of colleagues who display (in their view) positive attributes, negative attributes and indifferent attributes in this area and to write them down. The facilitator does not define or discuss equal opportunities at this stage. The names of these colleagues are written down on cards and given a number from one to six. The cards are shuffled and the participants are invited to draw out cards one to three. The facilitator asks them to consider reactions these three may have to given situations where equal opportunities is an issue. Who would do what and why would they do it? What are the differences/similarities? (The focus throughout the whole process is on what these colleagues *do*, not on what they *are*.) There then follows a closely supervised process of selecting people who are expected to show quite different reactions, followed by participants representing this on a prepared continuum showing, for example, attitudes ranging from open to hostile, supportive to unsupportive, tolerant to intolerant and so on.

Participants will continue and compare and contrast different combinations of senior managers. When each manager in this example has been included in six comparisons, it should be clear how each participant sees equal opportunities. A score can then be given to their comparisons, and so the repertory grid is constructed and used to reflect back at the individual and the group not only what the individual thinks about the issues, but what the group feels is best or most appropriate practice. The repertory grid process can be both complex and complicated. For evaluation purposes it is best kept as simple as possible.

Behaviour scales

These are used to establish what changes are expected from training and development actions and offer criteria by which these changes, if any, can be measured. Although admittedly patchy within individual institutions and across the higher education sector, staff appraisal offers an excellent opportunity to introduce behaviour scales. There is, however, not much evidence of the use of behaviour scales within the appraisal process anywhere in higher education

A simple example would be an agreed improvement in quantity and quality of publications. Development measures set in train at the appraisal might include some classroom-based activities (eg preparing to publish a course), assigning a mentor from within the faculty with extensive experience in publishing, reviewing time management skills in order to agree and establish research and writing time targets. The individual would then keep a record of how they felt they were improving, along the lines of a reflective journal or learning log that could form part of the individual's preparation for appraisal. This method offers the opportunity to make pre- and post-development action comparisons that have real and evident meaning for all parties. The organisation has, therefore, a clear 'audit trail' demonstrating the value of a development action (see Chapter 7).

A hypothetical example of the use of behaviour scales follows. The academic heads of department in one university were seen to be in need of developmental support to improve their interpersonal skills. Their academic background was, in the main, exemplary, but they like many others had been flung into the management arena, given a set of tasks, responsibilities and expectations and left to get on with it. Behavioural scales were selected as the most appropriate tool because the university wished to have some indication as to the perceived success of the training and development activity and also, given the highly political nature of the action and the cause of the action, to give it a high profile by involvement of a large number of staff at all levels.

The key stages
1. Staff opinions were sought via a survey. The questionnaire explored perceptions of managers' commitment to their staff and competence on delivering the requirements of their role. Questions on communication, consideration, man-

agement skills, teamworking, creating development opportunities, coaching, supporting, consulting were grouped together under various appropriate headings (at least ten in each category to enhance reliability) and respondents rated them on a five-point scale from 'never' to 'always'.

2. The academic heads were given a summary of the responses, expressed anonymously, as answers to the questions asked in the survey. They were rated on a five-point scale from 'agree' to 'disagree'. The feedback was discussed at academic board level and afterwards at a meeting of the academic heads with staff development, who had been responsible for conducting the survey and arranging the feedback.

3. A development programme was agreed. Part of this was to be classroom-based where there was a critical mass of low scores – as in financial management and people management skills – and part was via a raft of other strategies – mentoring, short secondments, exchanges inside and outside the university, team-building activities.

4. One year on, and following the end of the final session, a second survey was conducted and improvements – or otherwise – were then measurable. Chi squared percentages were used to compare the year-on-year changes.

The intended outcome was that there would be evidence of enhanced efficiency, and this was achieved. An unintended outcome was that there was a more coherent and cohesive working relationship between not only the academic heads themselves, but also with staff development.

Measuring changes in effectiveness

Measuring the impact that training and development actions have made should take place at three levels; organisational, departmental/team and individual.

Over the past few years the tendency by management in higher education to see the bottom line figure as the only real indicator of success or failure has served to impoverish the quality and quantity of staff development and training, in part because the units responsible for the delivery of development and training have not got clear systems linking what they do to what the institution wants and what it then achieves. For example, in pursuing its goal of achieving university status, a college of higher education ran a wide variety of training and development programmes for all categories of employees and the real spend on staff development had never been greater. However, there was no attempt either by management or by staff development to place a value on the increase in institutional status and therefore to link elements of that back to the training and development actions undertaken in support of becoming a university.

Looking at a far broader set of critical success factors has long been advocated. Blake and Mouton (1964) looked for high *production*-centred management practices coterminous with high *people*-centred management practices. Critical success factors can be used in an educational environment (see Chapter 11 for a description of how they are utilised by Gateshead College).

Bramley (1996) cites Cameron (1980) as providing a very useful classification of organisational effectiveness when discussing training and development evaluation with management. This also has potential value for higher education, in part for the reasons outlined above and also because it can be used in support of responsive evaluation as described in Chapter 4, and sits well with pay forward, tying staff development ever more closely to strategic management.

The four categories of organisational effectiveness

1. Goal directed
Here the focus is on output and achievement or otherwise of objectives, eg improvements in research ratings, training staff in the use of new software, improving communications.

2. Resource acquiring
Here effectiveness is assessed by the level to which the organisation 'acquires needed resources from its external environment' (Bramley 1996), eg research funding, grants, external contracts.

3. Constituencies
As the word implies, these are basically customer or client groups who are in some way stakeholders. Effectiveness is evaluated in terms of 'how well the organisation responds to the demands and expectations of these groups', eg audit and assessment, course and subject reviews, the research assessment exercise.

4. Internal process
The focus here is on aspects of organisational structure and culture such as stress levels, trust, information flow.

Bramley (1996) uses these categories as the basis from which to build a matrix, which is reproduced opposite as Figure 6.1.

	Individual (my work)	Work group (my section)	Function (my department)	Regional level	Organisational level
Goal directed					
Resource acquiring					
Satisfying constituencies					
Internal processes					

Figure 6.1: *Bramley's matrix*

These evaluation instruments are of great potential value if used with care and expertise, and can be applied with equal success to any category of employee. Constraints include time and resources. It is worth reiterating that the skills and knowledge needed to conduct the development, delivery and analysis do not always reside in staff development and/or personnel departments in universities and colleges.

Chapter 7

Effective Evaluation and the Investors in People Standard

'If you think training is expensive, try ignorance.'

(Drucker, 1993)

Any consideration of evaluation of training and development should include the Investors in People initiative. That is not to infer the national standard is the best or indeed the only way of improving the effectiveness of the training and development activity, rather that it provides a convenient instrument with which to address the issues set in the context of organisational objectives. The NCIHE (1997) recommends that:

'over the next year, all institutions should:

- *review and update their staff development policies to ensure they address the changing roles of staff; publish their policies and make them readily available for all staff;*
- *consider whether to seek the Investors in People award.'*

(National Committee of Inquiry into Higher Education (NCIHE) (1997) *Higher Education In The Learning Society*, Recommendation 47)

This chapter examines the considerable contribution Investors in People can make to understanding and developing evaluation as an essential tool of institutional and departmental planning and development.

The origin of the Investors in People is well documented, as is its current popularity within UK higher education. The initiative is taking off in Australia, with a number of pilot organisations currently being assessed. There is clear interest in the USA and about 60 other countries. In addition, an Investors in People UK funded project, managed by UCoSDA and including a number of UK universities and colleges, together with the Higher Education Quality Council, are putting Investors in People material onto the web with a particular focus on higher education. The objective is to provide the sector with user-friendly material set in a higher educator context. The URL is currently installed at Loughborough University at http://info.lboro.ac.uk/service/sd/IIPinHE2/IIPinHE2.html.

In an evaluation of some private sector organisations which have gained the Investors kitemark (Rix *et al*, 1994), it was noted that it is the *processes* within Investors in People which prove at least as useful to employers as the actual award itself. Most of the organisations in the early study had also considered Investors in People as being part of a Total Quality initiative. Rix also identified that a change 'champion' had been essential to the success of the Investors in People programme in all the recognised organisations. A common feature of recognised units and institutions within higher education is that there is a group of staff – a 'change team' – who diagnose, design and take action as appropriate using the Investors in People indicators as the basis for actions taken. Most of the recognised higher education institutions espouse a TQ philosophy. These in-house teams are often led by an internal 'project champion' or 'change agent' acting as the focal point, with external consultant(s) being used either very early on, at the 'mock' assessment stage or in an advisory capacity only.

Change management in higher education institutions is extremely variable. It displays strategies ranging between 'participative evolution' and 'charismatic transformation' (Stace and Dunphy, 1991). Consultation and collaboration with regard to the impact of change on strategic planning, the resulting institutional team and individual objectives and the staff training and development required in support of achieving these objectives is essential if training and development actions are to be understood and integrated seamlessly into institutional practice and procedures. In that way, any evaluative action will be seen as less threatening and will therefore have more relevance and integrity.

The fourth principle of the national standard states that: 'An Investor in People evaluates the investment in training and development to assess achievement and improve future effectiveness'. This will be explored in two ways. First, the evaluation indicators are linked to higher education. Second, the evaluation 'audit trail' is followed through the whole of the standard focusing on teams, individuals and organisational relationships with the evaluation process. See Appendix 3 for full details of the National Standard for Effective Investment in People.

Linking the evaluation indicators to higher education

4.1 The organisation evaluates the impact of training and development actions on knowledge, skills and attitude

Is there a system for evaluating if a particular training and development activity achieved the objectives set for it? (This should relate to indicator 2.6 in Appendix 3.) The assessor may look for evidence of evaluation methods and will expect something beyond the level of the 'happy sheet', such as targeted follow-up questionnaires, interviews, discussions with participants and their managers or even testing. How were outcomes of particular activities followed up? The method used for evaluating this 'learning' (ie the impact of 'training and development actions') is up to the HEI. It is also important not to overlook the importance of research outcomes and publications.

4.2 The organisation evaluates the impact of training and development actions on performance

Check that the training and development needs of the organisation, the team and the individual have been met (see indicator 2.4 in Appendix 3). A programme may have met its objectives, but has it made a difference? For example, a course on preparing for publication is deemed successful because the participants enjoyed it, the managers approved of it and it is in line with institutional objectives, but how many of the participants published? The assessor may look for evidence of evaluation against the training and development plans of the institution, team and individual. Peer observation of teaching could be a useful example here, providing the link is made between objective, training and development and performance improvement. How does the organisation evaluate whether the desired outcome of meeting that training and development need is achieved? Again, the system for evaluating the impact of training and development on performance is up to the organisation, but should be based on the objectives set at indicator 2.6.

4.3 The organisation evaluates the contribution of training and development to the achievement of its goals and targets

This indicator makes the link between 'the improvements in performance resulting from training and development actions'. Were the institutions' goals and targets met? Was performance improved and was the return on training and development realised? In what way do the results offer opportunities to further refine and develop institutional objectives? The assessor may look for evidence that the senior management or the senior decision-making bodies (such as senates, councils, academic boards, governing bodies) have reviewed the contribution of the training and development activity and taken action as a result. Locally, the assessor may wish to discuss how training and development activity is reviewed at team level. The institution will need to link its evaluation of the overall impact of training and development activities to indicator 2.2. Appraisal offers a useful example: as a result of the training for appraisal has the institution been more effective in achieving its objectives?

4.4 Top management understands the broad costs and benefits of training and developing employees

This does not mean that everything is quantified in money terms, but there should be an attempt to measure costs and benefits in broad terms and to plan ahead on the basis of this information. The assessor will expect to discuss this with senior staff. A strategy employing responsive evaluation measures would ensure these staff were already involved as stakeholders in the setting of objectives and criteria. They would also be able to describe how they received information 'bespoke' to their needs. The assessor may test this by discussing the understanding of the costs and benefits of training and development and how these lead to making judgements about future developmental activity. The HEFCE Higher Education Funding report (1995a) on quality assessment notes that one area where room for improvement was identified was the 'quality of academic management' and 'their effectiveness in communicating and developing good practice'. In essence, can – and do – key staff ask and answer these questions: 'Was our overall commitment to training and development worthwhile?' 'How do you know?'

4.5 Action takes place to implement improvements to training and development identified as a result of evaluation

The institution should take action as result of evaluation to improve those areas of its training and development activities where a need arises. This can apply equally to programmes (eg the introduction of IT training for curriculum development) or systems (eg where the appraisal system requires improvement). The assessor may follow through a sample of organisational, team and individual evaluations to see if the action points are fed into the next plan and acted upon. Has last year's evaluation made a difference? Clearly the process is ongoing and underpins the commitment to continuous improvement. The guidance notes for this indicator advise that 'this indicator should not lengthen the time required for an organisation to generate sufficient evidence for its first assessment' ... 'however at reassessment, all organisations will have had sufficient time to implement actions following an overall evaluation and will need to show evidence of this'.

4.6 Top management's continuing commitment to training and developing employees is demonstrated to all employees

Everyone should be told how training and development has contributed to the organisation's performance and publicity should be given to training and development achievements. This indicator is linked to 1.1 (see Appendix 3) and emphasises the fact that the actions of senior management should be perceived by employees to indicate a long-term commitment to developing people. This indicator will be particularly pertinent at the time of reassessment. Useful evidence here includes the recording, awareness or even celebration of training and development achievements. As a sector, higher education perhaps has more experience of this with regard to academic achievements in research and publications, and now needs to broaden this to embrace all staff. Of particular import to higher education at the moment is the expectation that evident commitment to training and development should continue through difficult times (or, as the 1996 Investors in People UK guidance puts it, 'adverse trading conditions').

(Adapted in part from Thackwray, R, UCoSDA Briefing paper 33 April 1996 The Revised Indicators Explained.)

The evaluation audit trail

The evaluation 'audit trail' starts with the business goals and targets (2.1 in Appendix 3) and their linkage to the objectives set for training and development (2.2 in Appendix 3). These indicators ensure that these objectives are being achieved. (This is what was hoped for, was it achieved? Rationalising the effect and the benefits after the event is not effective evaluation, but is commonplace within the sector.)

The organisation and evaluation

The assessor will look for evidence that the outcomes of the training and development are evaluated in terms of the learning that took place, and the direct effect on the organisation. It is *not* enough to describe the training activities and show improvements without demonstrating the direct link between the two. How were plans monitored? How were they changed? How effective were the changes? (See 2.3 in Appendix 3.)

The assessor will follow an audit trail starting with the broad aims (2.2) and/or the objectives (2.6), how the resource was used, through the action evidence to the evaluation of the effectiveness of that action (4.1) and the impact on the institution (4.3). This implies that the organisation must be able to demonstrate evidence through at least one planning cycle from the identification of need to the review at the end of the (academic) year, of the effect of training and development on organisational performance.

The assessor will expect senior managers to be fully aware of both the cost *and* benefits of the investment in broad but measurable terms (4.4). In larger organisations, such as universities and colleges, this indicates that it is necessary for information to be collated from evaluation conducted at team and individual level, as well as at the institutional level, to inform senior management.

'Pure' evaluation of the effect of training and development is almost impossible as there will always be a range of other factors that contaminate results, as noted in Chapter 3. Nothing is monocausal. Finally, the assessor will expect to see evidence from organisations that they evaluate the systems and processes and, where they can be improved and developed, that this evaluation is implemented.

Teams, individuals and evaluation

The purpose of this section of the assessment is to check the effectiveness of the training and development actions on the performance of individuals and teams and identify areas for further improvement. This time the 'audit trail' starts at one of two stages:

- when the training and development objectives are set at the identification of training needs (eg at appraisal or whatever other method is used to satisfy indicator 2.3); or

- at the pre-event briefing or discussion (2.6).

The assessor will check that heads of department, line managers, team leaders, etc have clarified the purpose of the agreed action, ie what the person or team was expected to do after the event that they were not able to do before (2.3 and 2.6). Did the action take place and can they now do what was expected?

The assessor will also look for evidence of post-event debriefing to check what staff *think* they can do and subsequent evidence that heads and managers monitor the performance to check whether the training or development action was successful. The assessor will ask what happens if performance does not improve. Is further training or development planned?

Taylor and Thackwray (1996) outline some common weaknesses concerning evaluation. These are listed below.

- A lack of clear linkages back to business objectives. This is often caused by poorly constructed business objectives, ie they are vague and perhaps not time-bound or measurable. Sometimes not all objectives are written down. For example, an academic department had as its main objectives, issues relating to refurbishment, new equipment, etc. Yet another imposition on already over-stretched staff – DIY?
- Sometimes evaluation evidence shows evaluation of the organisation's achievements and the outcomes of training and development, but fails to make a direct link between the two. Quite often it is very difficult to follow the audit trail. An assessor should be able to start at any point on the audit trail and trace the linkages back and forth.
- Quite often evidence is presented that shows pre-event briefings or discussion takes place and post-event de-briefings take place. What is missing is evidence showing how performance is monitored to check that the new skills or knowledge are being applied and are having the desired effect. Sometimes managers say they are monitoring the effect, but staff are unaware of it happening. Sometimes, as with research and innovations in teaching and learning, for example, there is evidence that new knowledge and skills are being used, but the information never reaches senior management or 'the centre', and consequently does not figure in overall evaluation activities and onward reporting.
- In many instances, senior managers understand the costs but not the benefits of training and development actions. This implies that expenditure on training and development has been an 'act of faith' and is bound to have an effect on the performance of the organisation, especially if it is very successful.
- In some organisations, especially larger ones like universities and colleges, line managers understand the benefits but senior managers evidently don't. This implies that a method of collating information about the effectiveness of training and development is needed and this information should be fed up to senior managers who themselves should require this as a matter of course.

Strategies for staff with people management responsibilities

To evaluate the effectiveness of the training and development the following questions need to be addressed:

- Did the training and development activity meet its objectives?
- Is the person (or team or organisation) now able to do what is required?
- What difference has it made to performance?
- What has been the benefit(s) of the training and development?

So what?

Those questions relate, in sequence, to the Investors in People indicators 4.1 to 4.4. After answering each question ask the question 'So what?' For example:

- The training and development activity met its objectives of helping trainees to learn a range of new skills. So what?
- Staff are now multi-skilled. So what?
- Staff are more flexible and can help colleagues to do other jobs. So what?

Clearly, the above process starts with a comparison between what was planned and what was achieved. Without objectives to compare achievements against, evaluation becomes at best subjective and often a rationalisation.

Another way for staff developers and managers to look at evaluation within the Investors in People paradigm is to paraphrase Kirkpatrick as follows:

- Did the participant enjoy the event?
- Did the participant learn anything?
- Was the learning transferred to the work situation?
- Did the department and/or the institution benefit?

Typically in higher education, the only questions asked are the first two. There is also a danger that they are not necessarily related to the reason the person attended the event in the first place, and therefore may lead to subjective evaluation or rationalisation. They cannot all be answered immediately – if at all. Evaluation must therefore be carried out in at least two stages: immediately after the event and some time after the event. Combining the first set of questions with the last set, therefore can lead to effective evaluation. An example of such a form is included as Appendix 2.

It is worth remembering that the Investors in People standard requires evaluation to be carried out at three levels: organisational, team and individual. In a large number of universities and colleges, autonomous units are seeking recognition independently. Where these units are very small, it will be difficult to separate the team and organisational levels.

When is evaluation effective?

1. At the end of the event

The first opportunity for evaluation of classroom-based training and development activities is at the end of the event, usually before leaving, and this process is therefore managed by the trainer or facilitator. Most facilitators of events, whether they are in-house or external, have some kind of evaluation along the lines of the reaction sheet. They are, as noted in Chapter 2, a potentially effective type of evaluation for a particular purpose. If constructed carefully they can give an immediate (apparent) reaction as to whether the participant *thinks* the objectives have been met. It is possible to encourage people to review the event by including questions about what they have learnt.

2. Immediate post-event de-briefs

It is very rare for some kind of de-brief not to take place at some level. This may often operate merely on the superficial level with most of the questions being *ad hoc* and probably concerned more with the enjoyment element and, perhaps, the cost. Learning and transfer possibilities might not crop up in the conversation. To make this a more meaningful exercise in evaluation, questions such as the following can be asked: 'Was the event successful in meeting the objectives we agreed before the event?', 'How will you use the skills/apply the knowledge that you have gained?', 'Do you now think you can do what we hoped you would be able to do which we discussed before you went on the event?', 'When should we review how you are using the skills and knowledge?'.

3. Later post-event de-briefs

Surprisingly few universities and colleges use this stage of the evaluation process. When asked how their manager knows whether the skills learnt on the training or developmental event are being used, a large number of staff simply don't know. Many managers, especially academic heads, simply *assume* that the skills will be used.

Very often they are, but this says far more about academic autonomy and self-direction than about evaluation and an institution's knowledge of itself. Others see that they are being used but don't acknowledge it. How long after an event it is worth reviewing the application of skills and/or knowledge depends on the complexity of the training and development.

If a group of people attended a post-event de-briefing, this can be used to contribute to evaluation at the team level as well as individual level.

4. Via the appraisal or training needs review process

To become an Investor in People an organisation needs a process to identify training and development needs, as discussed in Chapter 1. This process should offer an opportunity for evaluation. Training and development objectives will have been agreed at the previous review and they should be discussed, as should how the activity has impacted on performance, before any agreement is reached regarding new objectives. This is also the start of the process of gathering information about the benefits of training and development.

5. Learning logs (or similar)

Some higher education institutions have encouraged staff to keep learning logs. Although they can be seen as a bureaucratic chore, they can also be very useful in a number of ways.

They come in various forms and often link to individual development plans. Some staff may keep them as a record which will contribute to their continuous professional development. Several professional bodies require their members to keep such logs.

Learning logs are useful in that they enable the individual to review what has been learnt from training and/or developmental actions in a systematic way. How often have we returned from a conference full of good intentions which inevitably disappear under the volume of work that meets us on our return? The discipline of having a structured method of reviewing what was learnt and entering it in a learning log is a useful discipline to develop.

Unless there is a professional requirement, keeping a learning log is a discipline that is largely self-imposed. Institutions and departments that try to introduce learning logs as a policy often find that a large number of people do not complete them because they can be time consuming, especially if not done on a regular basis. It may, then, be better for organisations to agree the concept, the structure and the benefits rather than to try to impose it. In other words, secure agreement in advance of action.

Where Learning Logs are kept they contribute to evaluation at the individual level.

6. Achievement of qualifications, including NVQs

This is a very straightforward form of evaluation. When the outcome of training and development is the achievement of a professional, academic or vocational qualification this indicates that the objectives of the activity have been met and therefore contribute to the evaluation of the effectiveness of the training. What is then needed is evidence of the new knowledge and skills being *applied*.

The relative popularity of NVQs in higher education notwithstanding, the assessment of competence against National Standards through the NVQ process is another useful form of evaluation. However, it is also important when using NVQ assessments to illustrate evaluation, to be able to demonstrate what has been *learned* and how it has affected performance. In some cases the achievement of an NVQ may be merely confirming what the person has been able to do for some time, and little learning may have taken place. Although the achievement of the NVQ may have a motivational payback, especially for staff who have never had a piece of paper that says they are competent, the impact on performance may be marginal.

7. Sharing learning

Many higher education institutions require, expect or ask those who attend external development activities such as conferences to present a summary of the event to colleagues. There are a number of disadvantages to this method of training, especially if the 'presenter' is not trained in presentational skills. However, it may be reasonable to expect staff whose main function is facilitating learning (about half in most universities and colleges) to be able to use this approach effectively, and it can offer managers the chance to monitor what has been learnt, contributing to the evaluation of training and development.

8. Evaluation and project management

See Chapter 9.

9. Evaluation and continuous improvement

Learning through continuous improvement projects or groups may contribute to evaluation. It may not have always been planned to capture such learning, but with a little thought at the planning stage it should be possible to capture sufficient information about increases in knowledge and/or skills. Sometimes it is difficult to separate the 'learning' from other outcomes, especially if the improvement is focused on improved systems or processes, so that some aspects of learning will merely be implied.

There is often concern expressed about the bureaucracy of Investors in People and, without appropriate consideration, the evaluation process in particular can become very bureaucratic. It is therefore important to examine the processes that already exist and see if they can be used to help with evaluation. These processes can include quality assessment and audit, internal review and validation and many other measures currently employed by higher education institutions in answer to the question 'How well are you performing?' (see Chapter 8 and the Indicators of Programme Quality list produced by Mantz Yorke for HEQC).

A lot of the most essential processes mentioned above have been referred to earlier and, for those organisations working towards Investors in People, will therefore probably already exist or will have been introduced to satisfy earlier criteria.

With just a little tweaking they can be used for evaluative purposes. The process of de-briefing is easy to forget if it is not part of the culture or if heads of department are not naturally people managers. It is therefore advisable, especially in the early stages, to have a paper system which prompts managers to carry out these debriefs. It also enables organisations to 'audit' the post-training activity until debriefing becomes embedded in, and therefore part of, the culture.

Evaluating development

The evaluation of development is less tangible than training evaluation and is certainly more difficult. So how *do* you evaluate development?

There is no logical reason to attempt to evaluate every single developmental activity. Developmental activities can be clustered into 'programmes' or developmental projects. It is appropriate to use the appraisal or review process as the vehicle for setting aims and objectives and reviewing them, assuming the process is robust. For those institutions that encourage the use of personal development plans they would be the appropriate vehicle for evaluating effectiveness.

Agreeing and recording aims and objectives, and evaluating the 'development programme' is therefore a simple and unbureaucratic method of evaluating 'development'.

Evaluating the impact of training and development

Most higher education institutions find this is difficult to do, in common with most other organisations as the industrial society survey (see Chapter 11) confirms. The first question to ask is 'did the training and/or development have the planned effect?' This implies that there was a *planned* desired effect. Effective evaluation is checking *actual* outcomes against *planned* outcomes. There will, of course, be unexpected outcomes (hopefully beneficial) and these should also be acknowledged. The simplest approach to evaluation is based on having 'SMART' objectives at the planning stage, as shown below.

The 'SMART' objectives

- Specific
- Measurable
- Achievable
- Realistic and
- Timebound

An example of a SMART objective:

> By the end of the training and development action, the member of staff would be able to demonstrate that she or he has fully participated in the peer observation

programme by attending the briefing sessions, contributing to the development of small observation groups, arranging to both observe and be observed, agreeing informal feedback times, meeting as a group to discuss and identify development needs and suggested actions, and communicating this in summary form to the Head of Department for further action. Individual benefits will be discussed during the appraisal process.

This is as relevant at the organisational level as it is at the team and individual level, but possibly far more complex, given the size of most higher education institutions. It often means having some system for collating information gathered at team and individual level. Structured meetings could be used to pass information back up to the top about the effectiveness and benefits of training and development. These meetings may well already be established routine meetings. Whatever method is chosen it is important that it works. If the evaluation method doesn't work – change it.

Evaluation of systems

As Investors in People is linked to Total Quality and therefore continuous improvement it is important that the effectiveness of training and development systems and processes is reviewed, especially when they are newly established.

Managers and heads of department may wish to consider the following:

- Immediately after a person returns from an event, check what was learnt and whether the participant *thinks* the objectives agreed before the event were met.
- After an appropriate time, discuss with the participant whether the skills and knowledge are being used and whether the person is able to achieve what was expected prior to the event taking place.
- During appraisals or reviews check that previously set *learning* objectives have been met.
- Try to capture information about what has been learnt through project work or continuous improvement activity.
- Keep a simple record of benefits to the person, team or organisation so that it can be passed on to senior managers or whoever is responsible for collating such information at the organisational level.

In conclusion, it is clear that the significant tenet of Investors in People is its direct link with 'business' objectives. It has to be hoped that the development of clear objectives for the university or college, faculty and/or department and explaining these objectives to all staff – academic or porter, librarian or cook – will engender that essential sense of ownership via an understanding of what needs to be achieved and what every individual's contribution is (Thackwray, 1994). To date this corporate commitment within higher education has been rare – here or anywhere else. International experience based on Total Quality Management (TQM) programmes has been summed up by Piper (1993): 'Advocates of TQM have usually decided to ignore the President [Vice Chancellor], the faculty and other offices at least at the outset, to try TQM in their own units and attract attention through results. The "whole college" approach at Oregon State University that is, using full presidential support and a high level (in this case vice-president) champion, has been rare'.

The Investors in People standard cannot be achieved without clear evidence of commitment at the highest level; the Vice Chancellor, or head of any autonomous unit within a university or college which is aiming for Investors in People, will be formally interviewed by the Investors in People Assessor. The response will be set against other interviews over the final formal assessment. Investors in People recognition will not be gained unless an appropriate understanding of a clear corporate approach and its role and contribution within and to it is reflected by a critical mass of the staff.

The key Investors in People indicators are: 2.1–2.3, 2.6–2.7, 3.2–3.3, 4.1–4.5. See Appendix 3 for the details of these indicators.

Chapter 8

Learning From the Student Experience

'Education is what survives when what has been learnt has been forgotten.'

Skinner B F, *New Scientist*, May 1964

This chapter examines student assessment and evaluation. The links to developing a more effective evaluation of training and development are self evident. The level of detail that follows is primarily, but not exclusively, for those colleagues working in the training and development of staff who do not come from a teaching background.

It is evident that the various evaluation instruments, whether they are financial measures, such as transfer pricing (see Chapter 5), or whether they seek to evaluate changes in attitude or behaviour (see Chapter 6) are not greatly used within the sector.

The key question is, therefore, 'does that matter?'. Probably not, if what we do is appropriate for our purposes. There is, of course, much to learn from other sectors, but there is considerable achievement within our own. Consider how higher education approaches the assessment and evaluation of students. In particular, the focus in this chapter is on *learning styles* – the value of using knowledge of these when agreeing *how* learning is to take place has been referred to in several chapters.

Many higher education institutions readily admit to not having much idea of what, and importantly why, resources have been allocated to training and development either at the institutional or departmental level. Beneath this lies the evident perception of a need to improve the quality of management in higher education. Senior managers are sometimes either unwilling or unable to focus on the need for real data of both the qualitative and quantitative kind. However, peel away a further layer and there is a wealth of creativity, a considerable amount of local knowledge as to relative merits of undertaking a particular training or development action and, arguably, an excessive degree of self-criticism as to what else needs to be done.

Currently, higher education has to come to terms with:

- living with a diminishing unit of resource (see Chapter 5);

79

- the continued refinement of quality assurance practice and procedure;
- the evident need to improve the quality of management and management information within the sector.

Staff developers, trainers and budget managers need to show value for money in a recognisable way. Effective evaluation of training and development provides a framework to assist institutions in meeting these needs and demands. When discussing evaluation in the context of student performance, many colleagues have waxed lyrical about the systems practices and procedures that have been developed. However, this enthusiasm appears to wane when we start to apply it to ourselves.

A brief overview of teaching learning and assessment practices reveals a wealth of useful individual, departmental and corporate practices of great significance in evaluating institutional performance. A useful example has been prepared by Mantz Yorke (HEQC, 1996), where he lists the following in answer to the key evaluation question – how well are you performing?

Indicators of programme quality

- Student entry and exit numbers by mode and subject of study.
- Qualifications gained (against entry data if possible, this providing some kind of index of the value added to a student though participation in higher education, though this is methodologically difficult where programmes exhibit considerable diversity).
- Time taken by students to gain qualification.
- Continuation rates of students.
- The achievement of at least a threshold level of quality and academic standards (as revealed through the processes of quality audit [of assurance systems] and quality assessment [of academic provision]).
- Costs of providing programmes, on a per student basis.
- Institutional research performance.
- Institutional income generated from sources other than government.
- The financial health of institutions
- Institutional real estate (buildings and land).

Figure 8.1: *Indicators of programme quality*

How well are you performing?

As part of its training and development programme for HEFCE contract and subject assessors, UCoSDA has a produced a range of materials in support of enhancing understanding of the teaching learning and assessment process. One such example is *A Compendium of Principles for Developing and Enhancing Student Learning* (UCoSDA, 1994). The quoted text is in italics. The commentary serves as a link to staff development and its evaluation.

1. Guide the learner
Be sure learners know the objectives. Tell them what will be next. Provide them with organisation and structure appropriate to their developmental level.

Effective evaluation requires objectives to be set prior to any training and development actions taking place.

2. Develop a structured hierarchy of content
Some organisation in the material should be clear, but there should be opportunities for learners to do some structuring. Content needs to include concepts, applications and problem-solving.

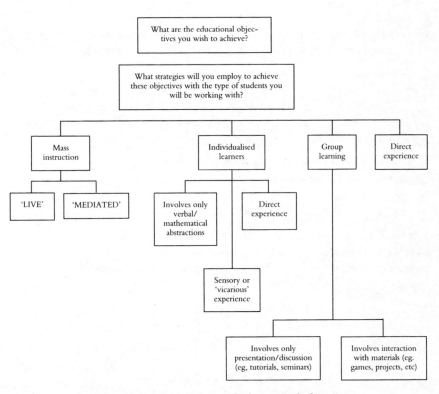

Figure 8.2: *Achievement of educational objectives*

Effective delivery of training and development actions in this context will effectively demonstrate that learning has taken place and that, with 1. above, it is in line with institutional objectives. To illustrate this further, see the summary diagram, Figure 8.2, widely adapted and re-used in teacher training programmes. The process *but not the language* occurs throughout the literature on evaluation.

3. Use images and visual learning
Many learners *prefer visual learning and have better retention when this mode is used. Encourage them to generate their own visual learning aids, eg charts, mind maps.*

4. Ensure that the student is active
Learners *must have opportunities to grapple actively with the material. This can be done internally through simply thinking and externally through writing and speaking on a topic and through practice.*

5. Require practice
Learning complex concepts, tasks or problem-solving requires opportunities to practise in a non-threatening environment. Some repetition is necessary to become both quick and accurate at tasks.

6. Provide feedback
Feedback should be prompt and, if at all possible, positive. Reward works better than punishment. Learners *need a second chance to practise after feedback in order to benefit fully from it.*

7. Have positive expectations of learners
Positive expectations of and respect from those delivering staff training and development *are highly motivating. Low expectations and disrespect are de-motivating. This is a very important principle, but it can not be learnt as a 'method'. It should permeate one's whole approach. Indeed, this impinges significantly on notions of academic level.*

8. Provide means for learners to be challenged yet successful
Be sure learners *have the proper background. Provide sufficient time and tasks which everyone can do successfully, but be sure there is a challenge to everyone. Success is very motivating. This may, at times, feel like you are being asked to manage contradictions!*

9. Use a variety of teaching styles
Use a variety of teaching styles and learning tasks so that each learner *can use his or her preferred style of learning and so that each* learner *becomes more proficient at all styles. Pace is an important factor to consider here.*

10. Make the class co-operative
Use co-operative group exercises. Assess group work as group work.

11. Ask thought-provoking questions
Not all thought-provoking questions have to have right answers but some answers may be better than others. Posing challenging questions can be particularly motivating for some learners (or for some categories of employee).

12. Be enthusiastic
Enthusiasm is motivating. One can learn to be enthusiastic and enthusiasm is a powerful motivator of learning.

13. Encourage learners to teach other learners
Learners who tutor others learn more themselves. In addition, learners *who tutor develop confidence and a sense of achievement.* Learning by doing, in other words. Work-based learning, peer support, supplementary instruction for and by staff.

14. Care about what you are doing
If you put teaching on 'automatic', then you cannot do an outstanding job.

15. Use different forms of assessment
Use a variety of assessment methods. Use criterion-referenced marking. Provide feedback during learning, encourage learners *to peer assess their learning.*

The University of Edinburgh's Teaching and Learning Centre has developed a checklist for observing a lecture. These are important and relevant criteria that the staff developer needs to consider when planning and evaluating an activity. Where appropriate the list has been slightly modified. Compare the suggestions to those contained in external (to higher education) guides to effective training and development practice, some of which can be found in Chapters 2, 3 and 5.

1. *Venue* Was the venue adequate – in terms of, for example, seating, lighting, heating, ventilation, audio-visual facilities, sightlines? If not, could the presenter have done more to help make the venue congenial? Of course, not all of these are the responsibility of the individual presenter and may well be outside their control. However, awareness of these issues is important.
2. *Content* Was adequate information available to the participants about the training and development activity as a whole? Were sufficient links drawn between this and other related activities such as appraisal?
3. *Structure* Was the material well-organised, so that the participants could follow the structure or sequence adopted? Were key points clearly emphasised?
4. *Level* Was the training and development activity pitched at a level the participants could understand? Was any provision made for those who experience difficulties?
5. *Clarity* If the training and development activity was classroom-based, was it clearly presented? Were the explanations given readily understood by the participants?
6. *Use of examples* Were examples of illustrations used whenever helpful to participants in grasping key points? Did the examples used engage with participants' knowledge and interests?
7. *Handouts and other materials* Where appropriate, did the presenter make appropriate use of handouts or other materials? If so, were these helpful in summarising, amplifying or reinforcing the presented material?

8. *Audio-visual aids* Were audio-visual aids used wherever needed in conveying the subject matter? Were the aids successful in supporting participants' understanding?
9. *Audibility* If classroom-based, could the presenter be clearly heard everywhere in the room?
10. *Pace and timing* Was the material presented at an appropriate speed? Was time effectively managed?
11. *Enthusiasm and interest* Was material presented in a lively and enthusiastic way? Was participants' interest in the subject material sustained or enhanced?
12. *Interaction* What scope was there for interacting with participants, eg by giving opportunities for questions or comments, or by drawing upon participants' interests, concerns or experiences?

Evaluating the effectiveness of practical sessions

The following checklist, adapted from the UCoSDA HEFCE Assessor Training Programme may be of help in evaluating effectiveness of practical sessions:

Clarity of purpose
● Was the purpose of the session explained clearly at the outset?
● Do the participants appear to know what they are expected to do?

Involvement
● Do the participants appear to know what they are doing?
● Are the participants involved in their tasks?
● Are only one or two in each group doing the work?
● Are the discussions amongst the participants
    (a) concerned with the task, and
    (b) indicative that learning is being developed?
● Are the participants observed at work?
● In discussion are questions asked which help their understanding?
● Are clear explanations of procedures provided?

The next chapter deals with project evaluation in general. Chapter 10 offers an example of project evaluation drawn from within higher education. Here, the focus is on the use of the project as an integral part of the students' learning experience. The material produced for the training and development of HEFCE assessors is of potential interest and value. The use of the project is widespread and crosses all discipline boundaries. Feedback and research indicate that, as a teaching technique, project methodology and delivery is particularly prone to problems for both lecturer and student. A closer examination follows.

Some essential features of effective development through project work can be summarised under the following headings:

- clarity of goals;
- explicit conveying of goals;
- careful planning;
- clear structure and communication;
- support with both the content and the process of working;
- explicit deadlines;
- help with time management;
- supportive, continuing supervision;
- explicit assessment criteria.

Learning and the learner

A learner-centred experience

A Quality Assurance Framework for Guidance and Learner Support in Higher Education: the Guidelines (HEQC, March 1995) includes a section on the experience of the learner. It divides usefully up into four inter-related sections covering entitlements, responsibilities and how these might be measured. These are shown in Figure 8.3 on page 86.

Approaches to learning

It has already been noted that planning training and development in terms of the learning styles of the participants not only improves the quality of the activity, but assists the evaluation process in that the interests of the participants as stakeholders have been taken into account. Knowing about – and using – approaches to learning, is an essential part of the staff developers toolkit.

Everyone has a different and ever-evolving approach to learning influenced by individual personality and learning style, the methods used and various environmental factors. The three broad approaches to learning in most common use are:

- The surface approach, primarily motivated by desire to complete the course and relying on memorising factual information, with a rote learning process, resulting in an outcome of mainly superficial understanding.
- The deep approach, primarily motivated by an interest in the subject, aiming for an outcome of thorough understanding of the material. This is usually achieved by one of three broad learning processes.
    1. The *operation learner* relies on logical, sequential approach, proceeding cautiously from one idea to the next.
    2. The *comprehension learner* aims directly for broad outlines of ideas, using analogies and fitting the knowledge into their own personal world view.
    3. The *versatile learner* combines both operation and comprehension processes, aiming for deep understanding buttressed by a sound factual knowledge.

Learners are entitled to:	Institutions are responsible for:	Learners are responsible for:	Indicative evidence might be:
• acknowledgement of their learning goals and requirements, expectations, personal circumstances and achievements:	• making arrangements for teaching and learning which enable learners to identify, review and achieve their learning goals;	• making use of the range of teaching and learning arrangements available to identify, review and achieve their learning goals;	• monitoring and analysis of the use of guidance and learner support systems by individuals and groups of learners;
• guidance and support systems that facilitate learning for both individuals and groups of students.	• ensuring that all learners have access to guidance and learner support facilities throughout their programme of learning, irrespective of length, location or mode of delivery;	• making appropriate use of guidance and learner support facilities throughout their learning programme;	• information from student feedback surveys on student expectations and experiences;
	• setting out the levels of service and support that learners can expect;	• giving constructive feedback on the arrangements available for teaching and learning, and for guidance and learner support.	• qualitative evidence including: learners' records of achievement; research into 'value-added', 'distance travelled' and achievement of personal learning goals.
	• collecting and acting upon feedback from learners about teaching, learning, guidance and support systems.		

Figure 8.3: *Measuring entitlements and responsibilities*

- The strategic approach is mainly motivated by the need to compete and better others, achieving recognition and using any process conductive to this, usually resulting in a variable level of understanding. These learners 'play the system' (Newble and Cannon, 1991).

Learning style characteristics

Kolb (1976) and Kolb and Lewis (1986) identify four types of learner (diverger, assimilator, converger and accommodator). Kolb's model of experiential learning, as shown in Figure 8.4, is cyclical and suggests that if learning is to be effective we need, at the *concrete experience stage*, to involve ourselves fully, openly and without bias in new experience.

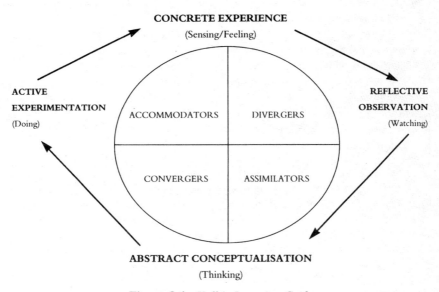

Figure 8.4: *Kolb's Learning Cycle*

The tables that follow look at learner characteristics in the form of strengths and disadvantages. They are categories of learner types, and the lists of characteristics are particularly helpful when agreeing training and development agendas with stakeholders – all of whom are (or should be) learners – and deciding on methodology and timing of reporting the results of evaluation. These lists are a useful tool in support of a responsive evaluation strategy.

Diverger strengths	Diverger disadvantages
• Imaginative thinker	• Frustrated by action plans
• Uses own experience	• Waits too long before getting started
• Looks at situations from many different perspectives	• Easily distracted
• Brings coherence to a mass of information	• Can be too easy going
• Sees relationships between things, grasps the whole picture	• Sometimes indecisive
• Wide-ranging interests	• Can't see the wood for the trees
• Good at listening and sharing	• Forgets important details
• Likes to get involved in the experience/information directly and then reflect on it	• Only works in bursts of energy
• Enjoys brainstorming and generation of ideas/alternatives	
• Likes social interaction/discussion/ group work	
• Aware of people's feelings	
• Wants to see the whole picture before examining the parts	

Figure 8.5: *Diverger*

Assimilator strengths	Assimilator disadvantages
● Precise	● Needs too much information before starting work or giving opinion
● Good at creating theoretical models	● Reluctant to try anything new
● Very thorough	● Likes to do things in a set way – lets go of the past reluctantly
● Sets clear goals	● Gets bogged down in theory
● Enjoys ideas and thinking them through	● Does not trust feelings – only trusts logic
● Analytical, logical	● Needs to know what the experts think
● Interested in facts and details	● Over-cautious, will not take risks
● Applies theories to problems/ situations	● Not very comfortable in group discussion
● Good at bringing different theoretical viewpoints to critique a situation	● Does not make use of friends/teachers as resources
● Examines facts carefully	
● Likes collecting data	
● Sequential thinking	
● Specialist interest	
● Avid reader	
● Move from parts to whole	
● Uses past experience constructively	
● See links between ideas	
● Thinks thing through	
● Well organised	
● Plans in advance	
● Enjoy didactic teaching	
● Happy to rework essays/notes	
● Works well alone	

Figure 8.6: *Assimilator*

Converger strengths	Converger disadvantages
● Practical application of ideas	● Intolerant of woolly ideas
● Decisive	● Not always patient with other people's suggestions
● Integrates theory and practice	● Resents being given answers
● Enjoys solving problems in a common sense way	● Tends to think their way is the only way of doing something
● Likes to try things out	● Needs to control and do it alone
● Feels happiest when there is a correct answer/solution	● Details get in the way sometimes – cannot see the wood for the trees
● Draws references from experience	● Not good at suggesting alternatives/lacks imagination
● Good at using skills and tinkering with things	● Getting the job done sometimes overrides doing it well
● Focuses clearly on specific problems	● Not concerned with presentation of work
● Able to see where theory has any practical relevance	● Needs to know how things they are asked to do will help in real life
● Moves from parts to whole	
● Thorough	
● Works well alone	
● Goal setting and action plans	
● Strategic thinking	
● Knows how to find information	
● Gets things done on time	
● Not easily distracted	
● Organises time well	
● Systematic notes/files	
● Reads instructions carefully	

Figure 8.7: *Converger*

Accommodator strengths	Accommodator disadvantages
• Testing experience, trial and error	• Tries too many things at once
• Committed to action	• Tends not to plan work
• Very flexible	• Poor time management, leaves things till the last minute
• Wide-ranging interests	• Not very interested in details
• Enjoys change, variety	• Does not check work or rework it
• Willing to take risks	• Jumps in too quickly without thinking things through
• Looks for hidden possibilities and excitement	• Sometimes seen as pushy
• Not worried about getting it wrong by volunteering/asking questions	
• Gets others involved	
• Learns from others, quite prepared to ask for help	
• Gets involved in something which sparks their interest	
• Uses gut reactions	
• Often gets right answer without logical justification	
• Wants to see whole picture before examining the parts	

Figure 8.8: *Accommodator*

Implications of learning style for learning and the evaluation of learning

What will be the impact on learning and its evaluation of staff perceptions of their own department, the staff training and development unit and the institution as a whole? Is this considered in the evaluation process? Entwistle and Tait (1990) and Ramsden (1991) have related styles of learning to students' perceptions of their departments. Findings indicate that departments where good teaching was reported were strongly orientated towards learning for deep understanding. Good teaching included such variables as effective lecturing, a reasonable workload, help with specific difficulties, useful feedback and perceived freedom to learn. Poor teaching included such variables as ineffective lecturing, heavy workload, inappropriate assessment and lack of freedom to learn. In these departments the orientation

91

towards surface learning was strong. *Reproducers* favour highly structured forms of teaching and assessment such as lectures and routinised examinations and assessments. *Understanders* work better in environments which provide some choice of what is studied, flexible approaches to teaching and learning, not excessive formal workloads and a variety of forms of assessment.

Styles of learning are more likely to be associated with a set of characteristics of a learning environment than with just one characteristic. Hence, to promote a particular style of learning it is necessary to consider the organisational climate of the institution or department as well as use of the various approaches to learning.

Assessing students: implications and lessons for the evaluation of training and development

There are many factors to be taken into account when judging the effectiveness of an assessment system for assessing students. The same can be said for various aspects of the evaluation of training and development. Effective assessment 'links closely with the learning objectives of the course, it assesses the central aspects of what is taught and learnt; it emphasises the development of deep, active, reflective learning; it focuses upon skills and their transfer; is efficient and comprises a reasonable work load' (UCoSDA, 1994).

Self- and peer assessment and evaluation

Self- and peer assessment and evaluation strategies have clear benefits including, notably, empowerment of the participant – it is not something that is done to them, rather it is their participation that promotes greater ownership, as was the case at the University of East London (see Chapter 10). Self- and peer assessment can assist with the development of skills such as team working, leadership and problem solving.

Below are some of the more common types of assessment of students, accompanied by a summary definition:

Formative assessment

Formative assessment is designed to diagnose student problems for the guidance of their subsequent study and assist in the learning process (eg diagnostic tests).

Summative assessment

Summative assessment is designed to inform decisions on the student's future (eg examinations).

Formative and summative assessment can be considered as a spiral, occurring continuously, giving a picture of where the student is currently at and where they need to go next.

Norm and criterion referenced assessment

The measurement element of assessment is normally classified into two types.

- *Norm referenced* assessment uses the results of all students to determine the standard used. In other words, students are assessed in comparison with each other (Cox, 1994). This practice is typified by the traditional examination system, the pass level being determined by the percentage of students given each grade.
- *Criterion referenced* assessment determines the criteria before the assessment, with the intention of ensuring certain minimal standards are met, or a minimal level of skill is acquired (Cox ,1994).

  The advantage of criterion referencing is in the objectivity, visibility and clarity of the process. A notable disadvantage is the need to compromise if too many students fail or, indeed, pass, as can be the case with professional examinations.

There is also *ipsative referenced* assessment, where the students are assessed only against their individual personal progress and development.

Significant weaknesses in the assessment of students include fuzzy or non-existent criteria. Assessment may be viewed by some departments as an extra rather than a recognised use of staff time, or the real time involved is not recognised.

Whatever type of assessment is used, there are three essential requirements: it must be valid, reliable and practical:

- Validity – does it measure what it is supposed to?
- Reliability – are the results produced consistent and replicable?
- Practicality- is it practical in terms of time and resources?
  (Newble and Cannon, 1991)

Here is further evidence that higher education has an abundance of skills in this area. The job of staff development, in tandem with management, is to incorporate these skills into a continuous evaluation and review process that is locally owned and understood largely because it is closely related to what staff are already doing anyway and does not look like a 'bolt-on' import.

Section 3 Evaluation in Practice

Introduction

'We recommend to institutions that they should develop a culture where each individual member of staff is aligned to the need to assist the organisation in becoming as efficient and effective as possible'

NCIHE Scottish Committee (1997) Recommendation 22

This section looks at a variety of practical solutions to the effective evaluation of training and development. In Chapter 11, examples are drawn from a range of institutions across the sector in the form of case studies. In Chapter 12, a variety of examples from organisations outside the sector are examined. Some of the organisations selected have been chosen because they belong to a sector where there are some similarities to the higher education situation, such as schools, further education and health. Others have been selected because they offer potentially useful insights into strategies and techniques designed to enhance effective evaluation.

All the organisations included have at some stage linked understanding the benefits of developing their people with improving the quality of what they do and/or produce, improving their relationship with their key stakeholders (both internal and external), increasing efficiency and effectiveness, and – most importantly – staying in existence. Hence they are learning to be learning organisations (see the Mills and Friesen definition below). The introduction to this section describes some key characteristics of a learning organisation.

What is a learning organisation?

The concept of a 'learning organisation' developed out of the self-development movement promulgated from the 1970s onwards, which clearly stressed each individual person's responsibility for addressing his or her own training and career development needs (Pedler, Burgoyne and Boydell, 1991).

In many cases people experienced this very positively, but all too often it was inflexible organisational structures, entrenched centralist policies or lack of recognition by the organisation of such self-development actions on the part of individual employees that acted as real barriers to self-development in practice. Gradually it was suggested that organisations needed to be open to, and value, learning for themselves as total entities: learning for organisations as well as learning for individuals in organisations. This idea was encapsulated in 'the learning organisation' literature from the late 1980s and continues to be very apposite today.

John Burgoyne (1992) has offered the following working definition of a learning organisation:

'A learning organisation continuously transforms itself in the process reciprocally linked to the development of all its members'. Alternatively, Mills and Friesen (1992) have described it as follows: 'We conceive of a learning organisation as one able to sustain consistent innovation or "learning", with the immediate goals of improving quality, enhancing customer or supplier relationships, more effectively executing business strategy, and the ultimate objective of sustaining profitability'.

Other definitions include 'A learning organisation is one that is continually expanding its capacity to create its future' (Senge, 1990) and 'A learning organisation harnesses the full brainpower, knowledge and experience available to it, in order to evolve continually for the benefit of all its stakeholders (Mayo and Lank, 1994).

The five disciplines of the learning organisation are:

- personal mastery – continuous learning by the individual;
- mental models – examining the way in which we view the world;
- building a shared vision – something that pulls everyone towards a common long-term goal;
- team learning – thinking together and producing results better than the members would on their own;
- systems thinking – seeing the relationships between all the components of the organisation.

Based on research from a number of organisations (Pedler *et al*, 1991), some eleven characteristics of a learning organisation have been identified that describe a learning organisation in practical terms (Burgoyne, 1992). These characteristics are listed below.

1. *A learning approach to strategy or policy:* whereby the very way an organisation decides collectively what to do and how to implement it, with ongoing monitoring and review, and adaptation of plans along the way, is itself a learning process.

2. *Participative policy making:* which involves as many people as possible in the policy making process, resulting in better local implementation and greater commitment and ownership of the plan(s), or as Burgoyne (1992) states, 'This may take much longer than it might when policy is decided by a small private group of people but what you lose in the extra discussion and thinking time you get back in the implementation time'.

3. *Informing: open information systems:* making key information available as widely as possible throughout the organisation, which supports participative policy making above but also provides the foundation for all the other characteristics.
4. *Formative accounting and control:* the provision of up-to-date information about the potential consequences of various actions in order to assist in local decision-making and in making changes in a more timely way.
5. *Mutual adjustment between departments:* the importance of each department or part of an organisation viewing itself as a customer of, or supplier to, another department or unit (emanating from a TQM [Total Quality Management] philosophy) and proactively working laterally with one another rather than only to top-down control.
6. *Reward flexibility:* having available within organisations the right kind of rewards and conditions for individuals in ways which reinforce learning.
7. *Adaptable structures:* possessing the ability to change structures and procedures relatively easily and cheaply.
8. *Boundary workers as environmental scanners:* the ability of organisations to learn about their environments from their *own* people, particularly those who interact directly with the customer at the internal (departmental) and external (client interface) boundaries.
9. *Inter-organisational learning:* the encouragement of everyone in the organisation to learn from everyone else, including internal and external suppliers.
10. *A particular kind of culture and climate:* which promotes learning, including positive learning from mistakes ('it's all right to make a mistake once, but it is not all right to make the same mistake two or three times'), and a leadership style that encourages taking some responsible risks but offers support and two-way communication throughout.
11. *Self-development opportunities for all:* whereby people have some degree of self-management and self-control over their own development and career progression, but that this self-development philosophy is guided, facilitated and resourced by the organisation.

Significantly, Partington (1994) has remarked that

> 'as organisations whose central purpose is the development of learning, it is paradoxical that universities have at present little claim to be regarded as learning organisations ... It is an irony that universities have within themselves arguably the richest resource of professional development expertise compared with any other organisations, yet they harness it only rarely and sporadically for their own most valuable asset – their staff.'

The NCIHE (Dearing) Report, *Higher Education in the Learning Society*, calls for universities to work towards being learning organisations – not least by considering the Investors in People process. The report notes that:

> 'A number of those offering us evidence commented on the irony that, in institutions devoted to learning and teaching and to the advancement of knowledge and understanding, so little attention is paid to equipping staff with advanced

knowledge and understanding of the processes of learning and teaching. Many see a need to rectify this situation.

Administrative and support staff are also concerned that they have little access to training and feel that their potential is under-used as a result.'

(NCIHE (1997) Chapter 3: Higher Education Today 3.41, 3.42)

Chapter 9

Project Evaluation

'It is the customary fate of new truths to begin as heresies and end as superstitions'

Huxley, T H, *Science and Culture*

Training and development can take many forms; eg coaching, shadowing, study leave, research, conferences, etc. Evaluating the real benefits of training and development requires a broad understanding of what it can comprise, as well as a shared definition. Consider the case of project management. Staff development itself can be described as a collection of projects reflecting institutional and departmental objectives, some running concurrently, some being 'grown' by staff development before being relocated in faculties and departments. This, however, is not how it is generally seen by most higher education institutions, sometimes causing concern and confusion.

In some sectors training and development is linked much more closely to project management, with clear purposes, clear methodologies and clear training and development activities in support of achieving those objectives over an already agreed timescale. In higher education staff development and training could benefit from seeing its function as essentially project oriented. The projects would stem from the strategic plan, which would have different priorities year on year. **Projects can be used to:**

- explore a topic more deeply;
- apply knowledge to a problem;
- provide training in research;
- develop initiative;
- foster independent learning;
- enhance time management skills;
- improve written communication of findings;
- improve oral presentations of findings;
- develop teamwork;
- develop leadership skills;

- analyse and synthesise, bringing new ideas to 'old' problems.

Apart from offering a clear structure and rationale to the activities of staff development, a project oriented approach would ensure that misunderstandings about role and function did not place staff developers in difficult positions. It can be difficult to 'let things go' having grown and nurtured them. For example, if peer observation or mentoring have grown through staff development, when the time is right for the activity to devolve to departments, an understandable concern with regard to 'what do we do now?' is often expressed. If the activity is seen as a staff development project, rather than the *raison d'être* of staff development it makes letting go easy, essential and logical as staff development moves on to the next project. This chapter looks at project evaluation in general, and the next chapter looks at project evaluation in practice.

Many organisations and training specialists outside higher education use 'SMART' objectives (specific, measurable, achievable, realistic and timebound; see Chapter 7). In assessing students, there are three essential requirements; validity, reliability and practicality (Newble and Cannon, 1991 see Chapters 9 and 5). Both have similar aims.

All forms of development should be planned and structured and should have a purpose, such as taking on new or different responsibilities in order to test potential or encourage creativeness. One way of giving it structure is to make the activity a 'development programme' or 'project'. This will be a series of linked activities each supporting or building on one another. For example, an Induction Programme is a development programme with the purpose of introducing new staff to the organisation (and the organisation to the new staff), its people and the individual's work. Induction often includes a training event as part of the programme; so too could other types of development programme.

All those being developed should be briefed prior to commencing a programme and the purpose and objectives must be agreed. As some development projects may be spread over a period of time, plans to monitor progress should be agreed with review dates entered in diaries accordingly. Initially, this may appear to involve additional work. If this does prove to be the case it is indicative of a gap. However, in many higher education institutions robust and rigorous processes will already exist and may merely need refining and – more typically – communicating.

Some organisations have 'improvement groups' or similar, that may be viewed as special projects. Although some projects may involve groups of people others may just involve one person. They may form part of the action associated with another learning or development opportunity. They may be associated with a specific qualification, such as an MA, an NVQ or a particular professional qualification. Where possible, accredit and follow up using existing systems.

Evaluating the learning from a project may not always be easy, but a properly planned evaluation strategy with learning objectives as part of the overall project plan will make the evaluation fairly straightforward and the results coherent and meaningful. The initial research involved in setting up the project is potentially a rich source of learning. External consultants could be brought in to support and enrich the activity. Throughout the project *learning* will be taking place at a variety of levels and in a variety of ways. Without planning for the unintended outcome much of this will not be captured. If it is planned into the project at an early stage it can contribute to more effective evaluation. A possible model is shown below. Although it begins with course/programme needs, the process can quite clearly begin anywhere.

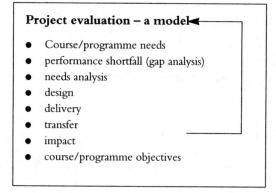

Figure 9.1: *Project evaluation – a model*

The following factors should be taken into account in evaluating the effectiveness of the project:

- major factors that helped in the achievement of objectives, eg senior management support, commitment of participants;
- those that 'got in the way' (prompts for future reference), eg lack of senior management support, funding arrangements;
- unintended outcomes, eg improved communication;
- enduring features, eg a positive change in the status of staff development;
- added value, eg improvement of student satisfaction.

The essential elements of project evaluation are summarised in Figure 9.2.
As with all forms of evaluation, the setting of criteria is of paramount importance. In essence, project evaluation lends itself particularly well to setting criteria, especially where groups of criteria are separated out into process and outcome criteria, as shown in Figure 9.3.

Project evaluation

- Project objectives
  - what was the perceived appropriateness of those objectives?
  - how successful were they in achieving targets?
- Project processes
  - perceived levels of success (the route, speed and mode of getting there)
  - were they the right processes?

Figure 9.2: *Project evaluation*

Setting criteria: assessment of process and measurement of outcomes

- Process criteria
  Construct a profile of skills requirements by identifying each key results area and then identifying the skills and knowledge required to achieve results in these areas. (It is then necessary to assess the extent to which these skills are being applied.)
- Outcome criteria
  Actions change the environment in some way. It is possible to assess these outcomes. The way this is done provides outcome criteria. This is the operational level (structure, system, resources, activities) of evaluation as actions produce operational results.
- Stakeholder agreement is essential

Figure 9.3: *Setting criteria: assessment of process and measurement of outcomes*

The final point, securing the support of stakeholders, is of paramount importance if project outcomes are to have any real value. For example, many universities and colleges have introduced some form of appraisal following a project, examining and testing appropriate models. Appraisal is, of course, an ideal vehicle for supporting effective evaluation. In a number of these institutions, after a year or two, it 'goes off the boil', to quote one senior member of staff in a new university. It is allowed to do so because key staff are aware that senior staff support for the appraisal process is largely rhetoric for the external audience, including assessors and auditors. They see it as another 'bolt-on activity' and accordingly give it a low priority. Had the support of all stakeholders been sought prior to and during the life of the project? What level of ownership was felt by staff? It is the involvement of stakeholders and enhancing ownership that form an integral component of the next chapter, looking at the evaluation of a staff development project in higher education.

Chapter 10

Evaluating Staff Development Projects in Higher Education: The QILT Project at the University of East London

'Curriculum design, assessment and evaluation begin at the same point'

Heywood, 1989

I have argued that staff development may be seen more as a series of inter-related projects emanating from responses to institutional and departmental plans rather than a continuous activity, and that involvement of stakeholders at the outset and throughout is an essential element of effective evaluation. The Quality Improvement in Learning and Teaching (QILT) project at the University of East London meets these criteria in so far as it is an organisation-wide department and team oriented activity involving staff at a variety of levels, and has as its basis the six core aspects of assessment. As the external evaluator to the project in 1996, I was impressed at the level of penetration of the principles and practice of QILT across the institution. Significant elements of the QILT Evaluation Report are included here in some detail as an example of the evaluation of a whole institution staff development activity using responsive evaluation instruments.

Quality improvement in learning and teaching (QILT)

The QILT Handbook (p 4) describes QILT as

'a process of continuous quality enhancement of learning and teaching which involves the creation, by staff groups (with the support of an Adviser), of Improvement Plans, their implementation, and the formative and summative evaluation of progress.'

The project developed in part out of the Enterprise Initiative, an April 1994 consultative document intended it to 'replace the triennial review process within the University's quality assurance procedures from September 1994'. An Educational Development Sub-Committee had been established in each faculty and a Head of Educational Development had recently been appointed.

Rationale

In terms of its own rationale, the QILT Handbook (p 43) offers the following:

> 'It is worth noting the comments expressed in the HEQC document *Learning from Audit* which reported, for example, that:
> - the extent to which teaching and learning is evaluated, both across and within institutions, remains variable and sometimes absent;
> - there was considerable variation in the way institutions collected feedback from students and employers;
> - the potential to share good practice is often limited.'

A link is made between the above and the six core aspects of HEFCE assessment, which provide the basis for the QILT funding process. All of this is encapsulated within the seven QILT Principles (below), thus making these principles the key instrument of the evaluation process.

Structure and operation

Working with an adviser, each department or subject team undertakes a regular cycle of quality improvement. The cycle has three phases.

Phase one – establish improvement plan
1. Identify issues from annual monitoring, student feedback, external examiner reports, and critical self-appraisal.
2. Establish an improvement plan which provides statements of areas where improvements are to be made, a timetable for achieving them, and an appropriate staff development programme.
3. Identify appropriate evaluation criteria and evidence to measure outcomes which might include: peer review; student feedback; products (such as open learning materials or videos); or observation of teaching.

Phase two – process of development
Undertake workshops, complete staff development, produce materials etc. Implement improvements such as: changes in teaching methods; changes to assessment; use of computer-based learning or whatever has been identified in the improvement plan.

Phase three – evaluation
Evaluate whether improvements have been achieved (according to the criteria established) and are effective and take action as appropriate. According to the QILT Handbook (pp 6–7):

> 'The exact level at which QILT projects shall be generated is difficult to define. Whenever possible it will cover all programmes and staff within a department. A large department, however, might cover more than one academically cognate subject area in which case there may be two, or even three subject groupings, each with a separate QILT programme. The same unit of evaluation shall be used for

annual monitoring and subject review. As far as possible the QILT groups will be representative of the HEFCE Subject Areas.'

The seven principles of QILT

The seven basic QILT principles were the central focus of the evaluation, the key indicators being that QILT and QILT-related activities had occasioned a greater knowledge, understanding and adoption of these principles.

'1. Quality in learning and teaching is central to the mission of UEL.
2. The goal is to improve the quality of learning.
3. Quality in learning and teaching depends on quality in learning, quality in teaching and quality in the context in which learning and teaching take place.
4. Teaching is a major aspect of UEL's scholarly activity and should be explicitly recognised and valued.
5. Improving the quality of learning and teaching is a whole-institution activity, impacting on every aspect of staff and student life.
6. The focus of any evaluation should be on the nature of the student learning experience at course component or programme level and not on individual students or staff.
7. The emphasis is on reaching consensus about what is meant by quality; definitions cannot simply be imposed as a managerial device.'

In effect, the project was to be audited in terms of general institutional impact and effectiveness, relating to the embedding of QILT principles into practice and procedure as perceived by the various stakeholders. A combination of activities was undertaken, as listed below.

- A short 'desk top review' of documentation relating to QILT, including both project-generated material and external commentary.
- A series of targeted interviews designed to determine the perceived effectiveness of the project with respondents being drawn from key players in three stakeholder groups: staff involved with QILT projects; other staff; students. This was, with the review day (see below), the major element of the evaluation process. The interviews explored the basic principles and operation of QILT and the report offers some reflections, on the perceived appropriateness of those principles and, more importantly, whether resulting activities underpin them, move the debate along, or suggest a re-think.
- A 'QILT review day' where a number of advisers and coordinators met with the QILT Coordinator and the Head of Educational Development. The purpose was to look at the progress of QILT and QILT-related activities over the past year and a half on an individual, departmental and corporate basis and to make recommendations for continuing to improve practice.
- The processes of the project were explored with a view to establishing their

perceived levels of success; in effect, the route, speed and mode of getting there. Were they the right processes?

- Feedback on the major factors that helped in the achievement of objectives, and those that 'got in the way', thereby producing prompts for future reference and consideration.
- Unintended outcomes, enduring features and added value – notably interest in QILT sectorally at the corporate, institutional and individual level, and internal impact on teams and team building.
- The decision to involve an external evaluator, from the Universities' and Colleges' Staff Development Agency (UCoSDA), in the evaluation of the perceived impact and effectiveness of QILT is clearly very much in keeping with QILT philosophy, practice and procedure. The relationship between QILT and staff development is explored later in this chapter.

Outcomes

There is clear evidence that QILT is attracting considerable outside interest. Significantly, this interest is not just confined to HEQC and HEFCE, where it could be argued that 'they would be, wouldn't they?'. A number of universities, old and new, are looking at QILT as a mechanism providing locally owned cross-institutional staff development. In addition, several colleagues have contributed to subject-related conferences and publications based on or triggered by participation in a QILT project. In talking with colleagues and looking through the literature it was evident that this is an unintended outcome and is a good example of added value as far as the staff are concerned.

In the outcomes listed below, where appropriate, the significant/most relevant QILT principles are indicated by numbers in brackets after the section number.

1. The students

1.1 (Principles 1–6) The Student Union has been involved from inception and clearly has an excellent working relationship with QILT staff. There is considerable paper evidence of participation in the various formal groupings where QILT was discussed, but more importantly, the Union feels it has been consulted adequately and appropriately at all stages in both formal and informal contexts.

1.2. (Principles 6, 5) QILT is seen as a successful medium for the enhancement of student participation in the evaluation and improvement of students' own academic development. In particular, some departments, notably Psychology, are thought to be excellent at involving students, QILT providing an appropriate vehicle for this involvement. Indeed, some of the comments relating to outcomes such as 'students advising students' have clear parallels with the US–originated Supplemental Instruction (SI) initiative active within many UK HEI's.

1.3. (Principle 7 – although not articulated as such) Where there were problems or difficulties encountered by students the view was expressed that these were largely to do with factors 'outside QILT'.

1.4. (Principles 5, 2, 1, 3) It was also felt that the 'grass roots nature' of QILT projects could be broadened to address other areas that contribute to the quality of the student experience, notably accommodation and communication, especially inter-site transport. Clearly all these are perceived to have an impact on the learning process as experienced by the students and are articulated in the HEFCE core area 'Student Support and Guidance'. Particular 'key features' include:

- the overall strategy for support and guidance,
- remedial support,
- pastoral and welfare support

1.5. (Principles 5, 4, 3) The view was also expressed that personal tutoring and learning support systems could be examined, perhaps via QILT projects.

1.6. (Principles 3, 5) There was also the perception that, whereas the Enterprise in Higher Education initiative had tended to have a more reactive, externally set agenda, QILT was enabling people to be more proactive in terms of contributing to enhancement of learning. Enterprise had part funded the Student Union's Education Unit and there is considerable traffic between this and the QILT office.

1.7. (Principles 1–7) The Students' Union is currently pursuing recognition as an Investor in People, with assessment provisionally arranged for August 1996. QILT presents, perhaps, an opportunity for the students to share some of the benefits of this experience with University staff.

2. The staff

2.1. (Principles 1, 7) Considerable evidence exists of the strong links between the quality assurance process and QILT. Originally, the QILT review process comprised annual monitoring and quinquennial subject review. It was felt that there was some trouble in convincing 'the university insofar as it would entail extra paperwork', underpinning the view that it should be done together. QILT is 'owned' by the Faculty Educational Development Sub-Committee (FEDS), not the Quality Sub-Committee which has responsibility for annual monitoring.

2.2. (Principles 4, 6, 7) Although there is, a general consensus that there are 'too many committees', there is also a measure of agreement suggesting that QILT projects and related matters are the province of those colleagues who develop, deliver monitor, evaluate and report on these projects and therefore have an entry in the business of all three Faculty Committees, as a 'locally owned institution-wide programme should have'. In some areas QILT may only be monitored by the Sub-Committees, but not actually 'owned' by them. An agreed (by all) model of good practice in this is the Faculty of Design, Engineering and Built Environment FEDS.

2.3. (Principle 1 – but 'central' is defined in different ways by different faculties.) Annual monitoring works at the departmental level (the preferred level) where there is a proper departmental focus. Where this focus does not exist, ie where it is 'pushed down' to courses or even individuals, departmental participation is reduced significantly. Consequently, there are still some staff with little or no knowledge of QILT and QILT projects in their own faculty. This is further exacerbated in some areas by the lack of meetings.

2.4. (Principle 7) Some academic staff think the status of QILT could be improved if the manager and coordinator actually taught on courses themselves. There is also the opposite view, that as the roles are ones of facilitation, support and empowerment this is not necessary. There was also the view that QILT was originally 'tainted' by seeming to be a formal teaching evaluation tool. That view seems to have largely died away now, like the opposition to observation.

2.5. (Principles 5, 4) There is interest amongst colleagues to learn why some departments have 'done nothing' and 'what happens to them if they don't'. This is further evidence of the sense of local ownership that was intended to be the hallmark of QILT. Colleagues involved in QILT projects express an interest in accountability – 'how do you know a good job has been done?'. Interestingly, the proactive stances demonstrated in the Psychology Department and the Faculty of Design, Engineering and Built Environment have met and answered this concern with regard to both students and staff.

2.6. (Principles 7, 1) In some cases it appears that QILT coordinators started with enthusiasm but found so many barriers to progress they became somewhat demotivated. This underpins the often articulated need for some broadening and formalising of the support available to these colleagues.

2.7. (Principles 1, 6, 7, 4) The links between QILT and appraisal currently appear to be tenuous. As both share the goal of continuous improvement, more attention should be paid by those staff responsible for the local delivery of appraisal – as givers and receivers – to ensure that impact and outcome of QILT-related initiatives is properly worked through as an example of individual personal and professional development. It may also be appropriate for the staff with corporate and faculty responsibility for staff development to ensure that this is incorporated into the appraisal training process.

2.8. (Principles 1, 2, 3, 4, 5, 6, 7) On several occasions the separate provision of staff development for different categories of employee was remarked upon. Most colleagues either felt that there should be one service for all, or that the issue was largely irrelevant to them. Those that felt there should be one service usually considered QILT an ideal vehicle to drive this forward. There were notable similarities between the staff and student views here, especially with regard to IT, English for Academic Purposes and other study skills related areas.

2.9. (Principles 7, 3) The University can be 'pushed around by external forces because we can't/don't/won't work together'. QILT is seen as positively contributing to the creation and development of a more team oriented culture which is perceived to be beneficial to the individual and the institutional community generally. This is particularly evident within Law where QILT is seen as having potential to 'bring people together to address particular issues such assessment and study skills development'.

2.10. (Principles 1,4) Colleagues remarked on the fact that specific funding was indicative of university support, the finance helping to 'buy time out'. They believe this 'time out' is repaid by improved teaching and learning practices and other benefits such as working in groups, publications and conference presentations.

2.11. (Principle 4) All colleagues placed great importance on the need to re-establish trust. QILT is seen as having (and currently in part fulfilling) this potential. It appears to offer an underpinning of professional integrity by empowering colleagues to manage their own development in line with the aims and objectives of the university – and the HEFCE.

2.12. (Principle 3) One important strategic concern was what, if anything should replace Enterprise. QILT offered the opportunity for teaching staff to be supported, for them to directly contribute to the enhancement of their courses, and for the agenda to be set at the local level. It also presented an opportunity to re-emphasise the importance of educational development as it relates to improving the teaching and learning 'culture'.

2.13. (Principles 1,7,4) The linking of QILT to research, via the RAE (Research Assessment Exercise) has been made by the university.

Conclusions and general comments

'There is currently no way to ensure that everyone who is invited turns up.'

'QILT helps practice to inform policy – and that is what should happen.'

'It legitimises what we are doing.'

'Budget surgeries available at appropriate times would be of great help.'

'QILT helps to get people out of "disciplinary dugouts" and "functional foxholes" and promotes the dissemination of good practice.'

'Review should be active and participatory and less paper based.'

'Staff need training in facilitation skills.'

'There ought to be more opportunities to involve the support services – helping to break down barriers'.

'Get rid of the TQ slogans/jargon from the guidelines and make them clear, firm but flexible.'

'We now do more self-evaluation, which is useful, although it wasn't intended.'

'It's all about let's see what you can do, let's see where the gaps are and what we need to do to fill the gaps.'

'We've got a really good idea here but some people don't want to play.'

Other evident institutional benefits (some unintended)

- Incorporation of QILT into corporate planning (staff development and training).
- Unifying university-wide strategic programme owned and managed at a local level but co-ordinated and supported at a corporate level.
- Raising the University profile – notably via HEQC, HEFCE, publication and conferences.
- Income generation opportunities.

Faculty/departmental issues

If participation in QILT activities is minimal or non-existent it is not evidence that nothing innovative or developmental is going. On the contrary, there is considerable evidence that a significant amount of work on improving teaching and learning is taking place. However, few colleagues outside the immediate group are aware of this, therefore the institution is impoverished. QILT appears to provide a means by which good practice is actively – and widely – disseminated (eg IT).

The reasons for non-participation have been variously described as 'systemic', 'eccentric', 'parochial', 'ideological'. The significant barrier was never related to QILT philosophy, practice and procedure. (There was one small exception, relating to the flexibility of the bidding process, ie it should be more flexible.)

Individual/personal/professional development issues

The impact of QILT is at its most visible here. No member of staff with direct involvement was critical or even particularly sceptical. The scepticism came from the 'uninvolved' colleagues, normally at a fairly senior level where, at least in one case, the view was that all the funding should be located in the faculties and should follow the research methodology with regard to funding allocation (ie by discipline). There is, of course, no reason why this can not be done within the current system, although local politics have clearly muddied the debate.

Recommendations

1. The University, and in particular the QILT office, Educational Development Services (EDS) and the relevant faculty groups and sub-committees, may wish to consider the following:

2. Good practice in using QILT as a medium for the enhancement of student participation in the evaluation and improvement of their own academic development (as perceived by the students) may well merit further examination and wider dissemination (eg Psychology).

3. There are clear parallels with the US-originated Supplemental Instruction (SI) initiative active within many UK HEI's. The University may wish to explore this further.

4. The 'grass roots nature' of QILT projects could be broadened to address other areas that contribute to the quality of the student experience.

5. The Students' Union is currently pursuing recognition as an Investor in People. The University, via QILT, may wish to draw on this experience as part of overall quality enhancement.

6. QILT projects could be used to examine personal tutoring and learning support systems (especially study support/skills and in particular English for Academic Purposes).

7. A set of performance indicators underpinning the seven QILT principles could be agreed, thus facilitating clearer and more focused evaluation.

8. Annual monitoring at departmental level may benefit from some tightening up in some areas.

9. The role of EDS/QILT management and coordination should be clarified further, especially with regard to teaching commitments.

10. The interest shown by individual colleagues in accountability reflects a concern for the different approaches adopted by – and within – faculties. Psychology and the Faculty of Design, Engineering and Built Environment offer useful examples of good practice here, and could be included in a revised QILT handbook as exemplars of good practice.

11. Consideration should be given to some broadening and formalising of the support available to QILT coordinators.

12. Existing and potential links between QILT and the appraisal process could usefully be explored.

13. More attention could be paid to creating and supporting projects that include staff other than those directly involved in teaching.

14. The bidding process could be re-examined with regard to its flexibility.

15. The relative merits of following the research methodology with regard to funding allocation (ie by discipline) might be explored.

16. The external impact of QILT could become a more significant element within the QILT aims and objectives, rather than 'added value' as it is now. A number of colleagues have contributed to subject-related conferences and

publications based on or triggered by participation in a QILT project. The QILT coordinator and Head of Educational Development have, in particular, made a considerable number of presentations to a variety of audiences across the sector, thus raising the profile of the institution.

QILT and staff development

In terms of its relationship with staff development, QILT depends on and supports:

- a coherent staff development policy covering the whole university;
- transparent criteria and procedures for promotion for teaching excellence;
- designated UEL staff development days;
- designated faculty or departmental staff development days;
- mandatory training for new staff;
- accredited and award-bearing programmes for staff who wish to achieve scholarly excellence as teachers;
- a management structure to deliver centrally sponsored staff development;
- funding to sustain a major developmental thrust involving all staff;
- specific funding to train advisers;
- proactive development planning by the Educational Development Committee and its sister sub-committees at faculty level.

In addition, QILT also aims to:

- provide organisational arrangements that enable more effective and efficient communication within and outside the University;
- enable organisations to break down the 'knowledge as power' culture which promotes secrecy, rumour-mongering and destructive gossip;
- enable participants to be open, honest, frank and informed about the University;
- enable definitions of quality to be determined in consultation with the 'stakeholders';
- provide definitions of quality which recognise realities of resourcing ('fitness for purpose' at a price);
- attempt to create consensus and commitment at all levels of the organisation;
- provide mechanisms for two-way accountability;
- replace retrospective deficit-focused review with proactive quality agenda and monitoring of current performance;
- facilitate a commitment to continual improvement.

The handbook claims that the resulting enhancing and monitoring of the quality of learning and teaching will impact on the activities of every department and the total student experience, including:

- mission, governance and policy;
- marketing and publicity;
- liaison and access;
- community links;
- admission and registration;
- finance;
- student support services;
- estates and accommodation;
- library and learning resources;
- management information services;
- audio-visual aids and technical back-up;
- computing and information technology;
- UEL-wide course models and management support;
- faculty policies and structures;
- management of integrated support for teaching;
- staff development.

In summary, therefore, QILT provides access and opportunity for staff to engage in developmental activities that they devise within parameters that, although set external to the organisation, are those to which the institution must work within and toward. The involvement of students in a range of ways produced interesting and valuable outcomes both intended and unintended. Staff development is locally owned and delivered. Stakeholders feel themselves to be included at appropriate levels and stages and evaluation is formative and summative, internal and external, with the results being fed back in to inform the next planning phase. There is a corporate budget to the activity and staff bid for funds, but the success of the activity is not specifically measured in financial terms, rather it is more appropriately measured in terms of the achievement of corporate/departmental/individual goals and objectives along the lines of the pay forward model described in Chapter 5.

Copies of the QILT handbook are available from Mike Laycock, QILT Co-ordinator, EDS, University of East London, Longbridge Road, Dagenham, Essex RM8 2AS.

Chapter 11

Outside Higher Education

'Comparisons are odious.'

Lust's Dominion, Act iii, Sc 4, Christopher Marlowe, 1565–1593.

In this chapter some examples of organisational approaches to evaluation are examined. A variety of organisations are included drawn from a variety of sectors. Some have obvious parallels in the type and nature of their activities, while others although totally different might well offer some useful insights. I begin with a broad overview based on a survey conducted by the Industrial Society. I am grateful to the Society for permission to reproduce some of their findings.

The Industrial Society Survey

In 1994 the Industrial Society reported the results of the Managing Best Practice Survey of 457 personnel and training professionals. The aim was to produce a current picture of the evaluation of training across a wide spectrum of organisational types. The topics covered included:

- responsibility for evaluation;
- commitment to evaluation;
- why the trend to evaluation;
- evaluation methods;
- training and development areas evaluated;
- measuring effects of evaluation;
- obstacles to evaluation;
- benefits from evaluation.

Most organisations employ someone whose responsibilities include the evaluation of training and development, but 19% of organisations surveyed carried out no systematic evaluation of training and development. Questions relating to the organisations' commitment to evaluation over the previous two years, as shown in Figure

119

11.1; as opposed to the following two years, produced a clear indication of an intention to increase, as shown in Figure 11.2 below.

Organisations' commitment to training evaluation – past two years

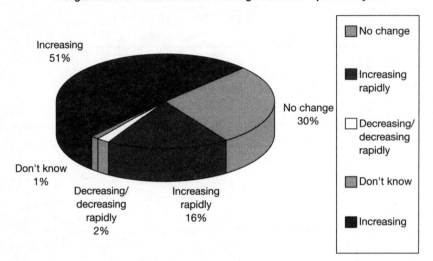

Figure 11.1: *Organisations' commitment to training evaluation, past two years.*
Source: Industrial Society, 1994

Organisations' commitment to training evaluation – next two years

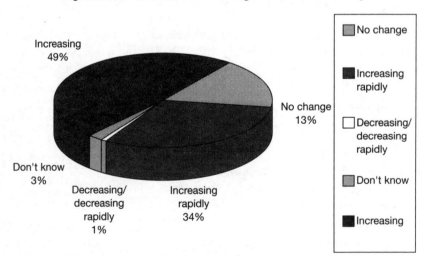

Figure 11.2: *Organisations' commitment to training evaluation, next two years.*
Source: Industrial Society, 1994

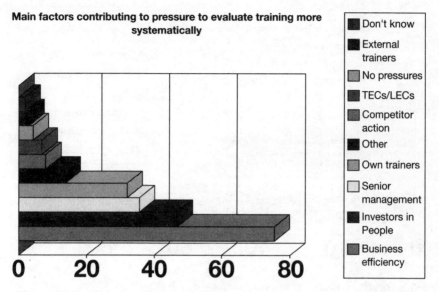

Figure 11.3: *Main factors contributing to pressure to evaluate training more systematically. Source: Industrial Society, 1994*

The survey showed that the Investors in People process was a significant contributory factor to the growth of interest in evaluation (see Chapter 7). Figure 11.3 describes a list of the main factors.

The reaction sheet was the most used form of evaluation, with 80% of respondents reporting use of an 'end-of-course trainee questionnaire', but only 14% reporting a follow-up line manager questionnaire. In contrast to other surveys, especially where senior management have been included, the area most subject to systematic evaluation is management training. Surprisingly, sales training is well down the list as shown below in Figure 11.4.

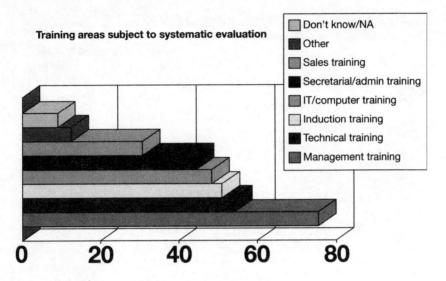

Figure 11.4: *Training areas subject to systematic evaluation. Source: Industrial Society, 1994*

The survey also confirms that organisations are extending their repertoire of ways in which they can develop staff, although the traditional classroom–based experience is still the most common, as Figure 11.5 shows.

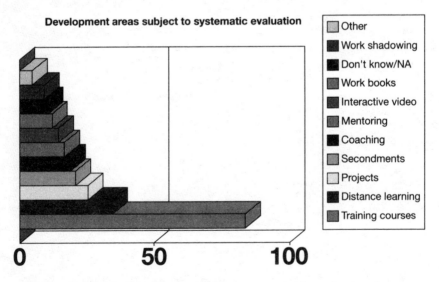

Figure 11.5: *Development areas subject to systematic evaluation. Source: Industrial Society, 1994*

The response to questions relating to evaluation methodologies employed is interesting, as more than half the respondents didn't know, as shown below in Figure 11.6.

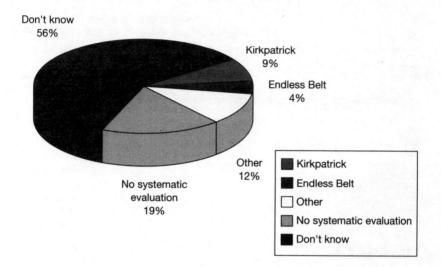

Figure 11.6: *Systematic methods used in the evaluation of training and development. Source: Industrial Society, 1994*

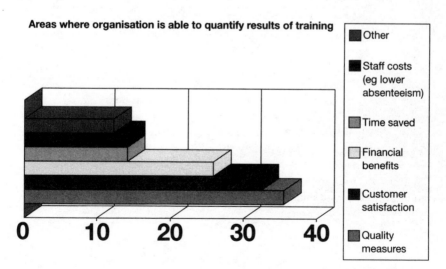

Figure 11.7: *Areas where the organisation is able to quantify the results of training. Source: Industrial Society, 1994*

Another problematical area for most organisations is quantification of impact. Quality and customer satisfaction are the two areas where quantification is more likely to take place as Figure 11.7 shows. (Interestingly, 37% of respondents selected 'don't know' in response to this question. This is not included in the Figure 11.7.)

Seventy-two per cent of the responding organisations were not able to put a financial value on training.

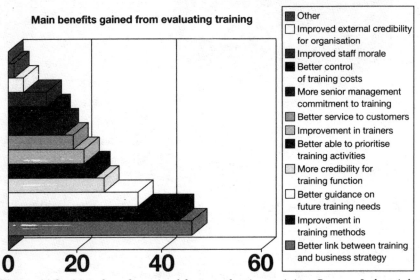

Figure 11.8: *Main benefits gained from evaluating training. Source: Industrial Society, 1994*

Finally, the survey looked at benefits and obstacles. It was clear from the results that one of the key drivers is the improvement of links between training and development and strategic planning processes. Interestingly, the survey also showed that most of the benefits rated, as shown in Figure 11.8, relate to the actual training and its supporting functions. (This may well be linked to the heavy use of reaction sheets and little else.)

With regard to barriers, the highest rated problem was the 'sheer difficulty of getting measurable results'. Figure 11.9 shows the list of main problems encountered.

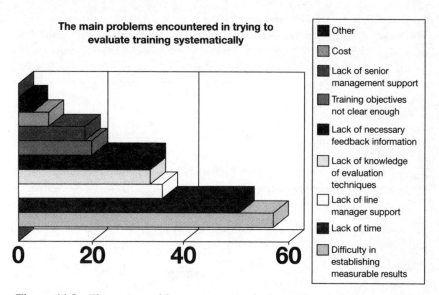

Figure 11.9: *The main problems encountered when trying to evaluate training systematically. Source: Industrial Society, 1994*

The organisations

1. Audit and Financial Services

Background
Audit and Financial Services is a division within the Directorate of Finance and Administration of Northampton County Council. The services provided by the division are:

- Audit and Consultancy (independent reviews of the full range of local authority activities as a management service);
- Exchequer Services (payroll, payments and pensions).

The division has undergone a number of organisational changes over the past few years. Six years ago staff were based in different parts of the former County Treasurer's department in County Hall. In July 1990 two separate business units were created within the Directorate of Commercial Services, Audit and Consultancy and Financial Services. Later, in 1993, the two units were combined into one division, Audit and Financial Services. Today, the division is located on one open-plan floor of a greenfield office block development and is within the Directorate of Finance and Administration.

Evaluation of training and development

The Head of Audit and Financial Services is responsible for the direction of the division's activities, being supported by the Chief Internal Auditor and the Exchequer Services Manager. Together, these comprise the senior management team. The division mainly provides services to the County Council, although some 9% of work is external.

The division's vision statement is:

- to be the best provider of payroll, pensions, payments, accountancy, audit and consultancy services;
- to satisfy our customers in ways which make us their first choice supplier;
- to achieve a level of financial return which enables us to invest in continuing to satisfy our customers.

The more detailed mission outlines what this means and includes the following under 'People':

- we must provide an environment which promotes the health, safety and welfare of staff;
- we must invest in training and development for both business and personal needs;
- we must give recognition for a job well done;
- we must develop staff as leaders in their specialisations;
- we must develop our understanding of our customers' needs;
- we must appraise people's performance formally, informally and regularly.

AFS has a 'Customer First' philosophy and divisional practice. The 'Customer First Document' contains three related elements:

- we must invest in training and development for both business and personal needs;
- we must give recognition for a job well done;
- we must appraise people's performance formally, informally and regularly.

This informs the approach to evaluation. Senior staff point out that 'the skills of our staff are vital to our success because our services depend on the efficiency of staff and on their relationships with the 'customers' to whom they provide services.

One measure employed is that of complaints. Figures had dropped dramatically, particularly in one area where some significant investment had been made to improve the team's efficiency. For example, one objective was to reduce the number of queries regarding accounts payable. In 1993, the figure stood at over 400, now there are about 40 at any one time. The Senior Management Team considers staffing and business performance issues at all meetings. When an objective has been achieved, team leaders recognise good work and offer positive feedback.

At the individual level, the outcomes of training are evaluated by observation by the team, by team leaders/section managers and via the appraisal process. At team level, particular problems, such as backlogs, have been dealt with and staff are able to connect the various stages of the process of evaluation.

At divisional level, senior management reviews organisational performance through targets, workflow, backlogs, etc. For example, personal computers were being introduced with concomitant training in use of spreadsheets and word processing. The outcome for one particular department was that the new skills were not being used much in their day-to-day duties, so the programme is being 'revisited' to ensure that the investment is realised. This was done via a computer training company offering training at a more broad and basic level as a means of securing the engagement of these staff.

The division was meeting and exceeding its financial targets in spite of budget cuts and staff reductions. The senior management team believes that this is due to the investment in staff, not only with regard to training and development, but also because of the delegation of the decision-making processes resulting in 'everyone having the opportunity to say what they think and be listened to'. In spite of financial pressures the training budget has not been cut over recent years.

2. HPC

Background

HPC was founded in 1960 in St Albans. Initially the organisation began by selling all forms of packaging, including self-adhesive tapes, corrugated cardboard and string. A close working relationship developed between HPC and 3M UK Ltd (now 3M UK plc). From 1965 the emphasis moved more and more to the distribution of the Scotch range of speciality tapes. The organisation became a preferred dealer and moved to Welwyn in 1977. Expansion and diversification led to a Basildon office being opened in 1984. The Welwyn and Basildon branches were combined in 1992 and relocated to Pin Green Industrial Area, Stevenage. Today the organisation stocks a wide range of self-adhesive tapes and adhesives and has its own slitting facilities. HPC achieved the quality 'standard' ISO9002 in July 1994. The organisation employs 18 people, over half of whom are dedicated to sales and sales support, and it is entirely owned by the Managing Director, his wife and the Sales Director.

Evaluation of training and development

There is a written business plan, setting out goals and targets. HPC devises and implements its training plan, reviewing and changing it on a regular basis.

HPC has an impressive array of evaluation instruments – especially so considering their size. A combination of strategy meetings, business opportunities reviews (culminating in a document circulated to all staff), reviews of a training goals and measurement form (HPC 141), and appraisals measure impact at all appropriate stages. The strategy meetings operate a continuous system of monitoring and review. An example form performing similar functions as the HPC 141 is attached as Appendix 13.

HPC evaluates the impact of training and development actions at several levels. They know if people enjoyed the activity (HPC 141), whether they learned anything (HPC 141, line manager review), whether the learning is being applied (HPC 141 follow ups, line manager observation, appraisal) and what the impact has been on the organisation (appraisal, strategy meetings). For example, at the individual level, a warehouseman worked out his own objectives (and had them reviewed over time) in consultation with the Administration Manager. A sales representative identified the need to convert more telephone calls to appointments. This need was met by 'dual working' with an experienced colleague and by attending an external course. An analysis of telephone call conversions was conducted before and after the exercise. With a further analysis later, improvement – and evidence of it – was monitored and sustained.

HPC spends 4.5% of its budget on training and development, with a specific element (1.8%) allocated for external programmes and activities and all staff are aware of what investment had been made in them by informal means (eg copies of memos/letters), and by inclusion of cost on their HPC 141s.

3. Queen Elizabeth's School

Background
Queen Elizabeth's School was established in 1573 and has been a fully functional school for 423 years. The original site of the school was in Wood Street, Barnet, and it moved during the 1930s to larger premises at its current location in Queen's Road, Barnet. The school provides for some 1100 pupils in the age range of 12 to 18.

The school is funded directly by the DfEE and is entirely independent from the Local Education Authority. Ultimate legal responsibility for the school lies with the governing body, while responsibility for the daily management of the school lies with the Headmaster.

There is a senior management team comprising ten senior staff who act as coaching leaders to the 73 full-time teachers who make up the teaching staff. There are some 30 support staff who work for the school in administrative, cleaning, catering or site/buildings capacities. The school is heavily over-subscribed and is ranked by OFSTED as being among the top 10% of maintained schools in the Public Examination league tables. In addition the school has a strong tradition of achievements in sport and music. The school mission is to produce boys who are 'confident, able and responsible'.

Evaluation of training and development
The school has a record of staff training providing a catalogue of all training undertaken since 1989 (the year it went Grant Maintained). The investment in training and development is controlled by the Senior Tutor who ensures that suggested development activities are in line with agreed targets and priorities. One of the clearest measures of performance improvement as an outcome of investment in training and development is the schools examination results. These have improved

markedly since 1989. The school is now in the top ten maintained boys schools as well as being in the top ten comprehensives in the country.

The school has a clear training plan, skills gaps are identified and measures are taken to close these gaps. The channel for these measures is the TKON system and, currently, the termly review with support staff. The TKON system is the measure used by the organisation to evaluate its development actions. The Headmaster is 'the anchor' of the system and all reports go to him. This is followed by analysis and further recommendations at Cabinet, the senior staff team meeting.

TKON is the schools' own organisational target setting and review mechanism, and comprises individual and group meetings with staff based upon individual's contribution to the school's mission. Goals are set, progressed and assessed in terms of the mission. (See the section on Gateshead College's Individual Contribution and development plan.) Although the system originally related to academic staff only, the school, following review of the current system for support staff, and as part of their commitment to continuous improvement, is establishing this as the system for all staff. The term is, therefore, no longer an acronym, rather it is part of the language 'currency' of the school.

An example demonstrating that development actions have achieved their objectives can be seen in the school's IT strategy. The objective was to improve efficiency via the introduction of the SIMS communication software. The school now holds a SIMS site of excellence certificate.

Training outcomes for individuals are assessed at TKON level and at department level. The Senior Tutor acts as a monitor of all training applications and related expenditure, and these applications also have to be endorsed by the department or subject heads and by the Deputy Head responsible for staffing. Examination results and applications for places are the key organisational level indicators. The boys themselves were seen by staff as an excellent indicator as to the effectiveness of their own training and development.

The governing body regularly receives reports on the costs and benefits of the development process. The Senior Tutor is a regular guest at governors meetings (as are most other senior staff and Cabinet members). The Headmaster has a formal target-setting meeting with the Chair of the Governors and regular reviews are held throughout the year. Proposals and costings of training are a matter of regular discussion. Managers are now expected to draft Departmental Development Plans which enhance performance in relation to the school's mission. The first question on the staff development programme application forms asks how the programme relates to the school mission.

The principal performance criteria (exam results, applications, the annual record of achievement and the size of the sixth form) are systematically relayed to staff through a variety of measures, both formal and informal. Formally, this is done through the weekly briefing (written and verbal) TKON/departmental follow ups, and governors meetings (there are two staff governors and usually other staff sit in on meetings).

4. Newnorth Print

Background

Newnorth Print has a product range which encompasses reports, brochures, maga-zines, mailers, price lists and stationery. The company evolved from Victorian beginnings as Henry Burt and Sons, founded in 1870. The 1960s and '70s saw major changes in the industry, and by the end of the 1970s the move from letterpress to litho was complete, bringing significant technological change. The company has invested heavily in the new technology and now offers what it calls 'the complete service'. It is currently one of the largest printing companies in Bedfordshire.

It has a broad customer base, with no single client accounting for more than 3% of turnover. Many of their clients have been with them for over 20 years. In 1989 Baldwin plc purchased the company. Baldwin has interests in three different sec-tors, printing, holidays and restaurants. The shares are listed on the London stock exchange (under leisure). Growth has been steady over the past few years and turnover is currently about £50 million.

Evaluation of training and development

As an autonomous company within Baldwin plc, Newnorth Print devises and implements its own training plan, reviewing and updating it regularly. It controls the resources that support training and development in the organisation. There is a formal review cycle addressing the business plan, with evaluation taking place twice per annum. This is supported by weekly management meetings where issues relat-ing to training and development actions are picked up. Profit generation and the reduction of costs are two significant measures used. The whole process is sup-ported by sophisticated software that monitors and evaluates performance across the range of activities. In addition, managers evaluate developments, particularly with regard to training with the new technology, on an informal daily basis.

All formal training is evaluated by the use of a post-course evaluation document. This is used directly after the training action as part of the debriefing, and is used again two months later as part of the objective checking exercise. Managers also evaluate one-to-one training on an informal basis via discussion between trainee and overseer.

The appraisal process offers evidence to the senior team as to whether develop-ment actions have achieved their objectives, and informs the planning and devel-opment process.

All the salient elements of the process have been recorded on appropriate docu-mentation such as the request for training form, appraisal information, the non-productive time summary, the individual production analysis and steering group notes, which are then used in support of the planning process.

Outcomes are evaluated at various levels. Overseers evaluate outcomes at the individual level, especially with regard to new technology. Processes originally introduced as part of ISO9002, initially seen as an imposition but now integrated into working practices, supported the evaluation process at the team and organisational levels. Training and development actions were followed up 'a long time after I'd finished, to see if it was useful'.

The appraisal process is the chief vehicle linking individual, team and organisation, and thereby informing and supporting the production of subsequent business plans.

The budget for training and development is determined by assessing individual training needs through the appraisal process and prioritising them against business objectives. The budget for training and development ranges between 1.5% and 3.5% of turnover, depending on business need.

5. Gateshead College

Background

Gateshead College, located in the North East of England, is one of the largest colleges of further education in the country. The location of the college is a depressed area, with the regional GDP being lower than the national average and with a very low number of businesses per 1000 population. Unemployment is high and increasing, particularly in the service and manufacturing sectors. Many people are leaving the area and the population level is in overall decline. A significant part of the population is in part-time low paid work. There are other large colleges in adjoining authorities and rivalry has been intense, although a merger is now planned with Newcastle College.

Evaluation of training and development

Evaluation of training and development at Gateshead College has the core business of the institution at its roots. This is achieved by outlining the delivery of the plan as Critical Success Factors. These are then translated into faculty and school objectives, and the individual training and development needs of staff in support of meeting these objectives are measured via an Individual Contribution and Development Plan. Its stated purpose is 'to provide a framework whereby training and development can be directly attributed to the achievement of both the corporate objectives (critical success factors) and continuous personal professional development'. The College is recognised as an Investors in People. The critical success factors are:

- student recruitment, retention and quality;
- business performance;
- quality;
- costs.

The structure and operation of the plan is similar to review and appraisal, and commences with a review between the individual member of staff and her or his line manager. This review checks and reinforces the individual's understanding and awareness of institutional and team objectives. In addition the Plan will demonstrate the link between what the individual actually does and institutional objectives; agrees and sets criteria by which progress towards agreed targets will be measured, and in so doing identify and agree training and development in support of this. The results of this process inform the structure content and delivery of the institutional training and development programme.

The accompanying documentation emphasises the importance and value of team and self-assessment not only in terms of achieving institutional objectives, but also enabling greater focusing of training and development actions on the individual staff members' personal and professional development. The critical success factors appear on the individual forms for guiding the discussion and planning process, as shown in Figure 12.1.

Driving up student recruitment, retention, achievement		
Agreed contribution (including dates)	Supporting evidence	Training/support required
eg teaching and learning, research and development,		
Drive up business performance		
Agreed contribution (including dates)	Supporting evidence	Training/support required
eg specialist knowledge and skills, industrial experience and liaison, research and development,		
Drive up quality		
Agreed contribution (including dates)	Supporting evidence	Training/support required
eg As above plus self-assessment, course management,		
Drive down costs		
Agreed contribution (including dates)	Supporting evidence	Training/support required
eg staff development, budgeting and marketing, course management		

Figure 12.1: *Individual contribution and development plan, Gateshead College*

Chapter 12

Higher Education

'Those who fail to learn from their history are condemned to relive it.'

George Santayama 1863–1952

As a sector, higher education favours the reaction sheet above all other forms of evaluation. This is in keeping with other sectors as shown in the previous chapter. This chapter follows on from that broad overview by offering a snapshot of some examples of the evaluation of training and development from within higher education. Some respondents focused solely on centrally driven activities, some focused mainly on classroom-based activities, all were asked similar questions relating to reaction, learning, application of learning, impact and perceived value.

It may be useful to reflect on the perception of evaluation of training and development in higher education by staff working in higher education. In June 1996, UCoSDA arranged the first national conference on evaluation of training and development. Speakers from a range of institutions from within and outside higher education offered views and descriptions of effective evaluation. The participants, staff and educational developers in the main, came from a variety of backgrounds, academic (teaching), academic (research), personnel and human resources. The group sessions, using a case study approach, producing some interesting reflections, and are summarised below.

It was felt that the sector might move towards developing more of a 'partnership in learning' with its staff, as follows:

- from being reactive, *ad hoc*, piecemeal training and development to strategic;
- from staff development unit as providers to facilitators and enablers;
- from evaluation of 'product' to evaluation of learning outcomes for the individual and the university.

Managers were seen both as the role models and key players. They should be considering:

- setting a broad learning agenda;
- translating it into success criteria;

133

- supporting the learning organisation within their immediate arena;
- needing to know what the outcomes are by:
  - collecting data systematically
  - seeking to understand it
  - feeding back to all involved
  - using the new understandings

It was seen as essential that institutions establish a common language and start asking such questions as:

- What are we really trying to achieve?
- How will we know when we've got there?
- How do we need to improve/extend our skills/capabilities in order to get there?
- What learning approaches shall we use to help us get there?
- Who/what do we need to enable that to happen?

Any emergent strategy would have to build in:

- clarity of purpose, continually refined;
- some precise success criteria, themselves challenged and redefined;
- a culture of learning for all;
- recognition of both long-term and short-term learning outcomes, a valuing of both.

All of this implies a major training need for managers throughout the institution.

Over the past two years I have interviewed a number of academic staff in a variety of institutions who have responsibility for staff development. It is their comments that, as noted in Chapter 1, suggested to me that the sector knows more about what it does and the concomitant impact on our work than we actually realise. This is evident in several of the brief case studies below. The results were originally intended to form a matrix, but responses showed a concentration at reaction level, albeit conducted in a variety of ways, with little evidence of consideration of evaluation of the impact of training and development on the institution. It might be more useful, therefore, to offer responses as 'snaphots', giving differing amounts of detail.

University of East London (UEL)

At the University of East London, evaluation takes place at several different levels with a focus on service delivery. All services are required to collect data to show whether they have met the agreed quality standards. Reaction sheets are reviewed and the outcome forms part of the Educational Development Services (EDS) Quality Standards report. In essence this report serves to set targets and standards, which are then approved by Central Services Quality Standards. Ultimately, recommendations are fed back to EDS.

The Quality Improvement in Learning and Teaching (QILT) project, the evaluation of which is described in some detail in Chapter 10, encourages departments to take on the responsibility of evaluating whether learning has taken place, via a report on the projects, incorporating some reflection on changes. The overall impact of QILT is evaluated through the scrutiny of the Educational Development Committee and via annual monitoring procedures.

EDS at UEL also, like an increasing number of staff and educational development units in higher education, have a rigorous departmental review. This takes the form of a self-evaluation report prepared by EDS and submitted to a panel comprising both internal and external members. Approximately 60 'stakeholders' are involved in focus groups looking at different aspects of the work of EDS.

EDS offer a postgraduate certificate for new academic staff and are now planning follow-up evaluation to assess impact some three years down the line.

University of East Anglia

At the reaction sheet level, UEA returns copies of the originals to presenters and analyses the contents to inform the process for future similar activities. This is especially applicable to induction and other long running programmes, and is seen to be less useful for 'one-offs' except where it is used to provide feedback on an external presenter.

UEA offers a women's development project (Springboard) and, in addition to the reaction sheet, offers a follow-up meeting for participants after three months which, with a written evaluation prepared by participants gives an overview of the quality of the programme and the impact it is having on the participants.

UEA has evolved a number of internal networks, for example, a group for technicians, Tec-net, and a group for secretaries, LinkUp 1–6. These and other groups arose in part out of appraisal, the in-house certificate in supervisory management and the Springboard programme, and they provide evidence of learning from training and development activities being used.

The university now uses the networks as consultation or focus groups, so there is clear impact on the organisation as people are clearly taking a greater responsibility for their own development.

The University of Bristol

All programmes have reaction sheets. These are sent to the presenters and are reviewed by Staff Development who respond to issues raised.

For follow-up evaluation selection criteria are applied, ie evaluation of expensive or extensive programmes, or innovative activities, or activities whose subject is currently under scrutiny, such as research. The follow up asks two basic questions, how has it (the activity) helped? What could we (Staff Development) have done better?

Buckinghamshire College

Both formative and summative measures are features of Buckinghamshire Colleges' approach to evaluation. The Staff Development Unit coordinates and facilitates meetings/focus groups at appropriate stages of an activity. This provides feedback which in turn is used as the basis for both formative and summative data. This practice extends to staff development in support of projects. One such example is the Career Management Initiative. The project aims to develop students' knowledge and skills in those areas which will enable them to secure appropriate employment, ease their transition into working life, and equip them to play an active role from the start of their employment. For staff and students this was a new venture with regard to structure, staffing (mixing academic and support staff), delivery and assessment.

Buckinghamshire College of Higher Education Strategic Plan (1996–2000) emphasises 'linked regional provision'. This was in line with Thames Valley Enterprise's (the local Training and Enterprise Council) Labour Market Research, focusing on the needs of SMEs taking account of National Targets.

An *ad hoc* pilot in 1994 aimed at reconciling regional SME requirements with students' career aspirations demonstrated the need for a more comprehensive initiative operating over different faculties and job markets.

In essence the evaluation format is responsive in nature. The rationale for the activity was agreed before any action was taken and it sat well both with the strategic plan of the college and its partner TEC. The objectives, therefore, arise from those plans and are reproduced below.

1. To enhance students' knowledge and skills in the key areas of:
   - personal skills audits, employment options and selection processes;
   - communication and problem solving in groups and teams;
   - relevant Information Technology applications;
   - relevant number/computational skills.
2. To optimise students' employability by developing:
   - awareness of their specific interests, aptitudes and abilities;
   - areas of special ability along with related knowledge areas and skills;
   - facility in job selection and interview processes;
   - knowledge and skills in areas which contribute to local SMEs (Small to Medium Enterprises).

3. To consolidate and further integrate links with regional employers by:
    - involving them in the planning, supervision, delivery and evaluation of the Initiative;
    - developing strategies and materials which could be used as a regional resource collection.

The evaluation of the project, therefore, could operate within clear parameters, and would:

- be both formative throughout the implementation phases of the pilots by means of feedback sheets, self-assessed tasks and observations, and summative by means of questionnaires and evaluator observations;
- also involve internal and external personnel.

In addition, each pilot maintains records of its planning meetings, reports of which are delivered to the Steering Group. The final report for each phase/year of the initiative will be compiled from the minutes of the Steering Group, along with the external evaluator's report.

In general evaluation at Buckinghamshire College places great emphasis on reflective practice. This technique, properly supported and developed, evidently sits more comfortably in a higher education environment than the more formulaic methods described in Chapter 5.

The Robert Gordon University

The university uses reaction sheets for all programmes. They are rated on usefulness and enjoyment. The scale is 1–5, 1 low and 5 high.

A system of 'highs and lows' is used for new events in the main, and enables the Staff Development and Training Group to evaluate projects from within the environment of a whole group where inhibitions may be less intrusive. Telephone follow-up evaluation methods may be used for the potentially more sensitive issues within the programme such as Stress Management Training and Assertiveness.

The university is also exploring the use of E-mail for evaluation purposes. Interestingly, this possibility was raised by their Investors in People assessment team. Other evaluation measures employed include:

- first destination statistics, ie student success rates;
- annual course appraisal;
- examples of any revisions that had been made to courses etc, eg revised time log from time management course;
- student course evaluation questionnaire.

The university runs a variety of follow-up sessions as a method of post-programme evaluation. For example, there are workshops on the results of time management, assertiveness skills and conflict handling events.

The Personnel Department has recently completed an exercise in Process Analysis looking at all the key processes, to ensure they are both effective and efficient. Where they are not, recommendations have been made, and action has been taken.

University of the West of England

The University defines staff development as: 'the acquisition of knowledge, skills and experience which will aid personal development and underpin the University's future development'. For each training programme, the objectives against which the programme can be assessed are established. These are stated in the documentation sent to delegates.

A pre-course questionnaire is sent to delegates to seek clarification of their personal objectives and other issues they are expecting to be included in the course programme. Participants and managers are written to, requesting that they meet and discuss objectives and evaluate the programme afterwards. When the programme is run on a modular basis, staff meet with the course leader during the programme to discuss progress. All delegates complete the post-course evaluation questionnaire. The reaction sheet is usually designed specifically for each individual programme.

If appropriate, a member of training and development staff attends at the end of the activity to conduct a verbal evaluation of the programme with the course leader not in attendance.

There is a discussion with the course leader focusing on the evaluation of the programme in the light of the written comments made by delegates. A sample group of delegates are informally interviewed to obtain direct feedback. This takes place quite soon after the event. Managers are then met with, particularly those who have larger numbers of staff, to review the training provision and the quality of the programmes. This happens at least annually, but may be more frequent depending upon the need. In addition, training and development staff attend departmental staff meetings on an *ad hoc* basis to assess future needs and obtain feedback from previous events.

Following the induction programme, a meeting six months after the course is arranged to obtain feedback as an additional follow-up. Delegates also felt that this would be a useful means of maintaining contact with each other.

On a quarterly basis a quantitative report is made to the Personnel Committee. On an annual basis, a more detailed report is made of what has been available and plans for the future. This meeting includes Governors and the Vice Chancellor. Repeat business is also used as an informal measure, ie when requests for further training and development are made – particularly by departments that were previously very unsure as to the value of the activity.

An evaluation of the effectiveness of the institutions' appraisal training programme undertaken and written by the personnel officer responsible for academic
related, administrative and all allied staff is included as Appendix 4.

University of Northumbria at Newcastle

The university defines staff development in terms of the type and nature of activity
that qualifies for some form of support. These are:

- *Post-Entry Training (PET)*: secondments; long courses of study or research leading to further qualifications; extended projects eg exploring new teaching and
  learning strategies; and where constraints allow, periods of sabbatical leave.
- *External Courses (ET)*: specific short courses or conferences (usually less than
  one week) or training events that take place away from the university and that
  are of particular relevance/importance/interest to the department and/or
  individual.
- *In-House Training (IH)*: any development or training activity arranged for
  groups of university staff by university staff. Some of these events will incur
  expenditure against faculty/department budgets. Others are arranged, as
  priority training events, as part of the centrally funded *Institution-wide Training
  and Development Programme*.

However, it is important to note that development need not always be a 'funded'
activity: job rotation, short secondments, work shadowing, coaching, for example,
can all reap benefits and require little funding.

The main focus of this case study is to describe the quality assurance mechanism
for centrally provided training and development programmes. The mechanism,
approved by the Training Advisory Group (TAG), for establishing the quality of
training provided under the Institution-wide Training and Development Programme (ITDP) is set out below. The information required for proposals for the
annual programme is detailed at Stage 1. Information required for the review of
training and development provided from ITDP funds will be reviewed using the
process described at Stage 2.

Stage 1 – commissioning the training/development

Once a need has been identified for training and development on a university-wide
basis, the Staff Development Section of the Personnel Department will commission
appropriate internal and external providers. When commissioning the following
guidelines will be adhered to:

- The training/development provided must be based on an analysis of need carried out by the commissioner, the provider or both.

- All programmes must have clearly stated objectives.
- Costs must have been presented to, and approved by, TAG.
- All programmes must include details of the participant feedback mechanisms and agreed evaluation methods to be followed.
- Consideration takes place, where appropriate, of whether the provider offers certification of training/development (eg NVQ, MCI [Management Charter Initiative]).

It is the responsibility of the commissioner to ensure that the guidelines above are followed and that the provider is made aware of the need to present a review report at the end of the programme (or at the end of the financial year for ongoing programmes).

Stage 2 – review report from the training/development provider

All providers of staff training and development activity funded by the ITDP should complete a short report (maximum two sides of A4) from which the effectiveness of the training/development provided can be assessed. Requests for the reports will be made in May of each year to be presented to TAG before the start of the new financial year in order to inform funding decisions for the following year. Such reports should include:

- Statement on what identified needs were met by the activities provided.
- Feedback provided by the participants (summary of the course evaluations).
- An evaluation of the programme against the agreed objectives.
- Details of any longer term benefits to participants themselves and their workplace as a result of the training and the method(s) used to collect this information (in order to disseminate good practice).
- Final costs for the programme(s) broken down into course/tutor fees, reprographic costs, hospitality costs, and any other costs. Reports should also attach participant lists/indicate the number of staff who participated in the programme.

UNN follows up the impact of training and development actions via some form of post-course questionnaire. The telephone survey questionnaire used by UNN to evaluate an IT development programme is attached as Appendix 5.

University of Nottingham

Organisational evaluation processes

Evaluation forms are issued at the end of all formal courses run by the Training and Staff Development Unit in order to gauge the reactions of staff and enable courses to be improved. The Unit seeks to evaluate the longer term impact of its formal courses through follow-up meetings and questionnaires. In addition to the above the university:

- undertakes regular surveys of all staff, approximately every four years, to ascertain the level to which the programme meets needs. Within this are questions seeking an individual evaluation of a training or development activity they have attended and to elicit a broad overview of the programme;
- uses specific approaches in the evaluation of certain programmes (eg institutional priorities, expensive ones). These may include NVQs undertaken externally by clerical and junior administrative staff;
- is developing methods of evaluating developmental processes such as mentoring. Mentoring is mandatory for new academic staff, it is evaluated halfway through the first year of the new member of staff's course and again at the end of the year. The focus is on the level of satisfaction the 'mentee' has with the level of support given. Mentoring at Nottingham is seen as a 'safety net activity', not in need of great formality. (On a broader front there is evidently considerable and growing interest in mentoring for new academic staff in British higher education. Further evaluative research is needed on the different models and their relative impact if mentoring as an institutional activity is to 'flourish in the longer term' (Blackwell and McLean, 1996));
- requires feedback on centrally funded activities. This fund is limited to support staff, whose feedback should incorporate commentary on how the course has benefited them and their ability to do their job;
- the university intends that the impact of training and staff development should be discussed in staff appraisal interviews partly in order to provide feedback to the Unit on the effectiveness of its programme.

In addition, the university intends that Promotion Committees should take into account both evidence of enhanced performance arising from staff development, and of contributions to the organisation and delivery of staff development at all levels.

Departmental evaluation processes

The university's Quality Assurance System recognises that Heads of Departments (and other units) have a managerial responsibility for training and development. In order to ensure proper planning and coordination of activities, departments are required to produce a staff development plan and to appoint a Staff Development Officer (who may be the Head of Department).

The Training and Staff Development Unit will provide assistance to departments, when requested, in developing and implementing their plans. In addition, the Unit will make available a fund for locally based staff development, to which departments will be invited to bid annually.

The university expects departments to encourage and support the involvement of individual members of staff in training and staff development activities (including by making appropriate time available) and, where necessary, to require it.

The evaluation of the effectiveness of study leave is an area that is not currently being addressed by higher education institutions. At Nottingham it is increasingly common for departments to require a written report and/or an oral report to a departmental meeting.

The Head of Staff Training and Development at the university conducted an informal survey of how study leave is managed and evaluated by departments. A summary of some of the findings follows.

- There is a university procedure on study leave and leave of absence when the absence is over a week within a term or a month outside of term time. Other than that, substantive policy is a departmental matter. In general, departments of all sizes have policies in this area, with one or two planning to introduce them. Very few departments gave negative responses, and where they did it tended to be in areas where other professional commitments caused complications.

- In the main, procedures are fairly formal, in the sense that they are written down and specify procedures and/or criteria in writing. A substantial minority of about one-third have informal systems that are not paper based. Many departments include comments in their unit staff development plan. Others have separate policies. The most impressive formal statements with clear criteria and operational procedures tended to be in the larger units.

- The commonest criteria for the allocation of study leave is by rotation every x years/semester. Most of those units and departments that specify a particular period of time, specify a semester. (This includes the majority of those favouring rotation.) Other departments decide on 'the merits of the case', sometimes explicitly taking into account the aims and objectives of the unit. For other departments and units the basis is competitive. Here, criteria includes the contribution to the schools Research Assessment Profile and states that priority should be given to staff who have just given up an onerous administrative or leadership role. In addition, there may be an explicit application procedure with selection based on merit following discussion at appraisal. One department had a points system based on length of service.

- Interestingly, only a minority of respondents actually said study leave is only available for research related activities. However, there were clear implicit suggestions that selection on this basis is commonplace. A few respondents commented on using the time for new developments and retraining opportunities.

- Monitoring and evaluation was more explicit than anticipated, although not particularly clear in some cases, usually where a rotational system was employed. Some departments include the need to produce a clear plan with measurable outputs. The requirement to report generally was commonplace. In some cases, staff discussed their plans prior to departure with the departments research committee and then met with them again on return to review achievements. (In other words, agreeing objectives for a development activity, setting criteria by which these will be measured and reviewing outcomes, as described elsewhere.)

- Departments are also responsible for evaluating the effectiveness of their peer observation systems, and the Staff Training and Development Unit is 'encouraging them to review on an annual basis'. There are checks as to whether the activity takes place to the level required via an internal audit mechanism.
- The university has a fund for departmental staff development. It funded over forty projects during the year 1996–7. Self- and peer evaluation of projects by oral and written reporting is encouraged by the retaining of 50% of the funding until a satisfactory mid-project oral report is received.

Individual evaluation processes

The University believes that training and staff development is likely to be most effective when individual members of staff take responsibility for their own development. It recognises that departments in particular will need to give appropriate support (including time), encouragement and direction to enable this process to occur.

The appraisal process has been revised recently. Staff development action points are recorded separately and, subject to agreement, they are then copied to the departmental staff development officer. In addition, most departments require some form of development log book and increasingly look to individuals to feed back on a cascade basis.

The University of Leeds

The university conducts extensive evaluations of specific training and development activities, such as its Postgraduate Certificate in Learning and Teaching in Higher Education. The results, which are discussed by the course advisory group and the staff-participant group, are used to inform practice for future programmes. Summaries are sent to the senior staff as appropriate and external examiners for information and action as appropriate.

University of Leicester

The university employs follow-up questionnaires some two months after the end of the training and development activity. All questionnaires, including the reaction sheet, are 'bespoke' to the activity – in line with the Kirkpatrick view (see Chapter 2). The Staff Development Committee is the formal reviewing body, although a number of 'stakeholder' advisory groups act as focus groups and providers of feedback. Currently there are clerical and technical advisory groups.

The university is also offering in-house accreditation for staff who, following the completion of a training and development activity, are observed in the workplace and assessed with regard to the use of the new skills learned and the concomitant behavioural changes. Although initially targeting clerical staff (it was the clerical advisory group that raised the idea initially) the process is clearly a transferable one and will eventually be open to all staff. A member of staff is currently being trained as an assessor.

Queen Mary and Westfield College, University of London

The college uses standard reaction sheets for all its training and development activities. Information drawn from the reaction sheets is used by the Office of Staff Development for institutional evaluation purposes. A summary is sent to presenters for self-evaluation purposes.

The Staff Development Adviser will often attend the summing up, at the end of each workshop to elicit feedback and in addition to obtaining detailed verbal feedback. The college is actively looking at further instruments and strategies to refine and deepen the process.

University of Newcastle upon Tyne

The reaction sheet is used to extract issues to address, items for improvement etc. The context is of significance, ie the type, nature and location of the training and development activity.

With groups where the agenda is experimental or developmental a surgery format is employed, enabling a more focused and specific evaluation to take place. Following the 'surgery' where a series of possible actions may have been discussed resulting in recommendations for action, a follow-up meeting takes place where the impact is evaluated in terms of:

- What did you learn?
- Did you apply it?
- Did it work?

Where the activity is certificated or accredited, the evaluation process comprises two complementary elements; a qualitative analysis undertaken by the Director of Quality Enhancement and a statistical analysis for the Boards of Studies. The qualitative material is used in case study format to support the quantitative data.

The Director of Quality Enhancement also self-evaluates his own delivery, along the lines of the Oxford Brookes model:

- What went well?
- What went less well?
- How will you change it next time?

The university will be conducting an internal review of its Quality Enhancement Unit in due course (the unit was formed in the summer of 1996).

University of Oxford

The university uses reaction sheets, which are currently under review. Follow-ups take several forms. At an informal level, selected responses are sought some two weeks after the end of a training and development activity. A more formal follow-up takes the form of a structured event. For example, twice per annum the university's recruitment and selection training runs a follow-up event where participants say what was useful, what has been difficult and what areas are in need of more thought/attention. In essence, how did it work in practice?

Subsequent programmes incorporate improvements stemming from the follow-up event responses. For some classroom-based programmes, such as time management, questionnaires are sent out three to four weeks after the event, focusing on the transfer of skills to the workplace.

University of Hull

All information drawn from the reaction sheets is acted upon, and feedback is communicated to those areas that support the training and development activity, such as catering. Currently, staff development has two MSc students looking at aspects of the evaluation process, and an additional student testing out evaluation software acquired from Humberside Training and Enterprise Council.

A staff development report sent to the staff development unit and provided by faculties and departments is used as a basis for the consideration of further funding allocations and contains a review of impact and effectiveness of training and development actions to date. The report also includes a summary of issues that came up during the appraisal process.

Particular programmes are selected for more detailed follow-ups. One example is the Staff and Educational Development Association (SEDA) accredited General Management Skills, open to all staff with a management responsibility.

Sheffield Hallam University

Here, the University is trying to move away from the number crunching activities, such as counting the number of people participating in a training and development activity and assessing the cost, towards systems that are measurable and/or demonstrable. It is planned to agree evaluation measures in advance of any training and development action and review outcomes against identified measures. The key question is 'what is the organisational or performance improvement you want to see from the activity?'. For example, a research related target might be to raise the number of publications. The means of achieving this will vary from area to area and from individual to individual, whether it be working with senior researchers or participating in a structured programme. A demonstrable benefit would be an improvement to the research rating.

There is an increasing focus on the involvement of managers as developers of staff. A key priority for the institution and the Staff Development Unit is to work with managers locally to help enhance their evaluative skills. A resource pack on systematic approaches to staff development activities is being prepared for the start of the 1997–8 academic year. It aims to support managers through the staff development process from identifying a need for the monitoring and evaluating of training and development actions. The pack will be supported by practical 'hands-on' workshops.

A template has been produced to assist the recording of quantitative information arising from training and development actions such as costs and time.

For seemingly unquantifiable activities like mentoring, or activities where no direct costs are incurred, managers will estimate the hidden costs involved by assessing the number of hours the activity will entail. In this way, managers will gain a greater understanding of real costs involved in the whole range of activities undertaken.

Managers are encouraged to discuss expected outcomes with staff prior to development activities and evaluate the actual experience against these afterwards.

University of Bradford

The university places an interesting and positive emphasis on team/peer evaluation. For example, at the reaction level the delivery team is brought together with other key stakeholders for an immediate review of what went well, what went less well and what areas are in need of some attention. Evaluation at all levels is placed in the context of strategic planning. This is best set in the context of the decision-making process and organisation of in-house staff development as follows.

A range of external factors, notably the HEFCE and the HEQC, set the national funding and quality context. The university sets academic and business objectives, including quality targets. That process completed, it then informs the departmental setting of academic and business objectives and QA targets. Departmental meetings are held where the staff development implications are discussed. This in turn feeds into the appraisal process where individuals will decide their own training and development needs. Individuals and/or Heads of Department discuss these emergent needs with their staff development advisers who then set in train the various actions relating to nature, style, timing, etc of the training and development action agreed, including the setting up of a staff development team to design and plan the training and development action. Clearly, the training and development action is firmly located in the context of business planning. Evaluation, therefore, is assisted at several levels. At the individual level there is the report back to departmental meetings; the staff development team evaluates the outcomes and reviews the programme; this is then fed back to appropriate committees. In terms of the resourcing of the activity, the staff development sub-committee decides resources and priorities on the basis of the university's agreed academic and business objectives, which in turn informs the staff development advisers' decision-making process.

The University of Hertfordshire

The university defines staff development as including 'everything that is done by and for staff in order to maintain and extend their work-related knowledge, skills and capabilities'. The *purpose* of staff development is seen by the university as having two interrelated strands:

- to encourage and support all staff to achieve individual work and career goals;
- to enable and assist all staff to make the most effective possible contribution to the aims and objectives of their faculty/centre/department and to the university as a whole.

The policy commits the institution to the monitoring and evaluation of staff development activity 'so as to continually learn and improve provision'.

The policy also states that staff development involves a cycle of activity: planning, delivery, monitoring and evaluation. The results of evaluation are taken into account and acted upon for the next stage of the cycle. The Staff Development Unit undertakes a thorough monitoring and evaluation of its work. An annual audit and report of its activity is prepared by the SDU for Academic Board and senior management. The complete policy is attached as Appendix 6.

One interesting example of the university's evaluation strategy is the questionnaire on the first year of the Professional Development Programme in teaching and learning in higher education, which uses an Optical Mark Reader (OMR) answer form.

Part A of the questionnaire seeks a response on personal details, course details and university matters such as library and other resources, student services etc. Part B of the questionnaire is the Ramsden Student Experience Questionnaire, widely used in research into learning in higher education. The questions are based on comments that students have often made about their experiences of higher education teaching. They have been specially chosen to reflect aspects of courses that are generally important across a wide range of disciplines. Finally, part C covers questions about the staff delivering the programme. Parts A and C are completed by all students on *any* accredited University course, part B is optional. The questionnaire is attached as Appendix 7.

In its Enterprise in Higher Education Quinquennial Review the university notes that 'the present rate of change in HE is such that it threatened to overtake us even with the benefit of Enterprise. Academic staff development therefore becomes even more of a priority than hitherto if we are to continue to deliver quality courses. Academic Audit, Quality Assessment and the Investors in People programme will inevitably result in an increased need for staff development and again, an academic network is needed to deliver this.'

As to the evaluation of the Enterprise initiative, the university notes that 'evaluation has been a continuous process, the evidence for it coming in various forms and from various sources, including quantitative and qualitative monitoring data, reflective analysis, anecdotes and informed opinion drawn from students, staff, employers and others'. Extracts from the staff development and evaluation sections of the Quinquennial Review are attached as Appendix 8.

The Open University

The Open University has been developing its evaluation of training and development over a number of years. It has a fairly sophisticated system which seeks to assess not only reaction but also learning and the application of that learning. The longer term evaluation questionnaire is 'bespoke' to each programme but follows a similar format. The questionnaire divides into three sections: A. Content of the course; B. Personal development and application of course to work; C. Contribution of course to job performance, unit and university objectives.

A. Content of the course
This section asks questions relating to the topic in tick box format with four responses ranging from highly relevant to not relevant. There is a chance to expand on the response categories 'of limited relevance' and 'not relevant', and a further opportunity to reflect on content in terms of inclusion and exclusion based on work experience since the end of the training/development activity.

B. Personal development and application of course to work
There are three questions in this section. The first asks respondents to rate themselves in terms of their current ability against each of the programme objectives on a four-point scale from confident and knowledgeable to not confident or knowledgeable. The second question seeks a response on how respondents have applied their learning, and the third question looks for feedback on debriefings with line managers.

C. Contribution of course to job performance, unit and university objectives
As the title suggests, this section elicits feedback on participants' perception of benefits accruing to them and their own performance, the contribution the programme has made to achievement of departmental objectives and benefits of the programme to the Open University generally.

The university also seeks feedback on perceived effectiveness of local induction from new staff through a questionnaire seeking responses relating to role and function, responsibility for induction, mentoring arrangements, general support, the value and use of the guide to induction and professional development and the open workshops (free-standing introductory units where attendance is optional).

This list of examples of approaches is neither exhaustive nor exclusive, rather it reflects where higher education is generally located with regard to the evaluation of training and development. Some institutions have developed evaluation strategies designed to look at whole institutional issues. One example is the University of Central Lancashire. Here a pro forma is completed by all budget holders. The completed document provides information on the investment in 'personal and professional development' for an academic year. It includes details of actual expenditure by category of employee, a record of appraisal completion dates and a summary of identified priorities. These priorities must be confirmed as being consistent with the faculty or departmental plan. Another strategy, focusing on stakeholders, is employed by the University of Teesside. Here focus groups are used to review activities, look at particular issues arising and make recommendations accordingly.

Chapter 13

Conclusions and Reflections:
A Model for Higher Education?

'Not everything that counts can be counted
and not everything that can be
counted counts'

W B Cameron

'Do You Know What You Are?
You Are What You Is'

Frank Zappa

In the introduction it is suggested that an appropriate model for higher education would combine the strengths of the *pay forward model* and the flexibility and political sense of the *responsive approach* to evaluation. For any model to have significance and value for higher education, it must encourage the application of existing skills, strategies and techniques. A TQM cliché exhorts us to 'play people to their strengths'. The same is true for higher education. Collectively, higher education has the knowledge, experience and skills to effectively evaluate its activities to its own and its stakeholders' satisfaction. The systems it is invited to use, however, do not 'fit'. The language is wrong, the techniques often relate only to instructional training. Academic autonomy, integrity and self-direction is compromised if subject to inappropriate evaluation measures. That higher education is 'different' is indisputable, so although the various evaluation instruments described in this book can be used, they should be used within those systems that higher education actually uses. 'You can't organise this place like the others' (Major-domo of Brittany, 1703).

The key message is to agree what the core business of the institution actually comprises. This means sweeping away the rhetoric and replacing it with a clear and understandable (jargon-free) statement describing:

- This is what we do
- This is how it works
- This is how we check it works
- This is what we do as a result of that check

When the nature of core business is agreed (eg teaching, learning and research) all staff can be made aware of what it is that they do that contributes to what the organisation does. Departmental and individual objectives can then be set in the context of agreed and understood and relevant institutional objectives.

Some thoughts and issues in developing a workable model for higher education (or: A case for the accreditation of practically everyone?)

1. Define staff training and development for the whole institution

Agree what is included and what is not. For example, if study leave/scholarly activity is included how is it evaluated and at what level?

2. Agree a training and development cycle

The training and development cycle must be agreed with all appropriate stake-holders and be firmly located within the institution's strategic planning, aiming for a seamless join between management and development. Each institution should seek to develop its own model, based on its own definition of what staff development comprises, but there will clearly be areas of commonality. Taylor and Thack-wray (1997) produced a simple working model, the extended training and development cycle shown in Figure 13.1, that can be used as a starting point for discussion locally and institutionally. The language can be changed as appropriate, (changing 'business' to 'institutional', for example) and timing of the stages can be wrapped around significant events and activities such as audit and assessment, the appraisal process, committee, meeting and reporting structures.

The systems, techniques, strategies and criteria applied to the assessment and evaluation of higher education programmes can be applied to the continuing professional development of all staff, in line with a responsive evaluation strategy and the learning organisation definition: 'A Learning Organisation harnesses the full brainpower, knowledge and experience available to it, in order to evolve continually for the benefit of all its stakeholders'. (Mayo and Lank, 1994)

3. Discuss and agree the setting of objectives, targets and standards for training and development activities

Many of the difficulties associated with effective evaluation arise because higher education institutions are poor at both setting and keeping to objectives. Poorly constructed training and development objectives are usually vague. Vague objectives are not objectives but broad statements of what is required. (eg, the objective for the next research assessment is to do better).

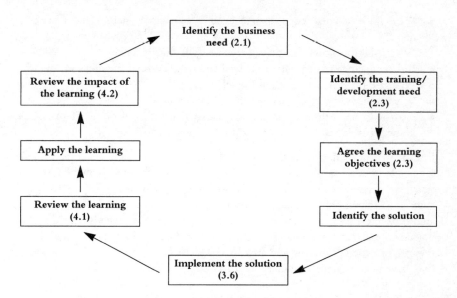

Figure 13.1: *The extended training and development cycle (the numbers in brackets are the relevant Investors in People indicators). Source: Taylor and Thackwray, 1997*

The following example actually occurred within a UK higher education institution in the mid-1990s. The porter whose job it was to deliver the internal mail was always late and getting later. Without consultation, his manager sent him on a basic time management course. The departmental objective was to see that 'the mail arrived on time. Following the course his timing did not improve, it got worse. He was spotted by a senior member of staff taking a rubber band out of a large bag of rubber bands and tying it around a wheel of his trolley. When asked why he was doing this he said that the wheel kept falling off when he went up and down stairs and he had been told by his manager that there was no money in the kitty to repair it. *What was the real training and development need and for whom?*

Clearly if objectives are not clarified staff may well participate in 'wrong' or irrelevant training and development activities. Setting the criteria for learning in advance is therefore very important (see Figure 13.2).

The outcome of defining and agreeing what staff training and development means to the institution, and establishing a training and development cycle, will have ensured that planning for evaluation of training starts with institutional or departmental needs and objectives. Put simply, these objectives should answer the following questions:

- What is the institution/department trying to achieve? (If you don't know what you want, how can you know when you've got it?)

- What skills or knowledge do staff need to help in the achievement of these objectives?
- What skills or knowledge do the relevant staff already have?
- Is there a gap between what is needed and what current capabilities allow for?
- What are the learning needs of the relevant staff?
- What is the best way of meeting these learning needs?
- How will the institution/department know that they can do it? (If you don't know what you want, how can you know when you've got it?)

For the staff developer or the manager, objectives can be made clearer and more specific by simply asking and answering the following question: 'How will I know when the person demonstrates the new skill or applies the newly acquired knowledge?' Sometimes objectives may exist in the mind of some of the stakeholders but are not written down, discussed and agreed. It may be acceptable to agree verbal objectives, but there is less room for misunderstanding, or political manoeuvring if they are recorded in writing and circulated widely. Evaluating whether the objectives have been achieved is much easier to do if they have been written down.

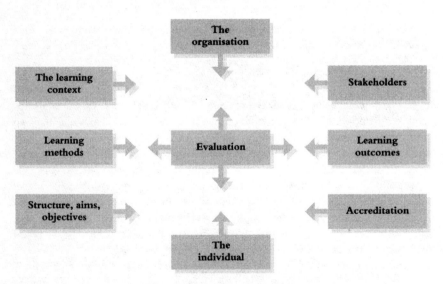

Figure 13.2: *Setting criteria*

4. Consider the peculiar position of academic staff

There are currently no formal qualifications required for people entering the higher education sector. At the time of writing there is a general consensus that if the sector does not agree a system enabling nationally recognised professional accreditation of higher education teachers, one will be imposed from outside. It is increasingly being seen as inappropriate and anomalous for a sector that does so much with regard to the professional training and development of other professions, not to have

154

a clear, recognisable and transferable system for itself. Indeed, there is currently no formal qualification required at entry or for progression. The NCIHE Report (1997) reflects this concern:

> 'In Chapter 8 we made clear our belief that higher education teaching needs to have higher status and be regarded as a profession of standing. To support this we have proposed the establishment of a professional Institute for Learning and Teaching in Higher Education, one of whose roles would be to accredit programmes of higher education teaching training. There is widespread support for a system of accreditation, as our staff survey and the responses to our consultation indicated.'

NCIHE Report (1997) Chapter 14, Staff In Higher Education, 14.28

Encouragement by senior staff to undertake such development on a voluntary basis is evidently rare. There is a scheme developed by the Staff and Educational Development Association (SEDA) offering accreditation to 'new' higher education teachers. Institutions submit their programme to SEDA for approval. Programmes must meet the SEDA values and objectives and must be externally examined and moderated. Uptake is not high, either in terms of total participating individuals or total participating institutions, and appears to be concentrated within post-1992 universities. SEDA is a voluntary body and its programme depends on voluntary commitment. There is little formal requirement for involvement with the host institution's quality assurance systems, so opportunities for the involvement of all the key stakeholders at the outset are severely restricted. Consequently, the professional training development and accreditation of this group of staff by this route will tend to remain separate from the strategic management of the institution, thereby weakening its overall impact individually, institutionally and nationally. A deliberate effort must be made by the institution and the department to discover whether the newly accredited learning is being used post-accreditation, and to determine its impact.

Individual institutions design, develop and deliver their courses and programmes to a wide variety of undergraduate, postgraduate, professional and vocational students, and are subject to rigorous monitoring, evaluation and review. There is no reason why the training and development of academic staff cannot be approached in the same way. A flexible modular structure with a significant distance learning element, quality assured by the institution's own procedures and leading to a (transferable) qualification would provide an appropriate system of accreditation not just for new academic staff, but for all staff in terms of keeping up with new techniques, improving skills and knowledge and so on. Peer observation and appraisal would be significant elements in the process. I have argued that the effective evaluation of staff training and development in higher education depends upon the sector's ability to draw on its existing strengths. This is especially significant with regard to academic staff. It is inappropriate, therefore, merely to suggest that all programmes should be accredited and evaluated using existing quality assurance systems without providing some suggestions as to how this might be (or is being) achieved.

In order to maximise the quality of academic provision in teaching and research, many initiatives found to greater or lesser degrees in a wide variety of institutions can systematically be linked. This would provide opportunities for quality improvement and continuing innovation at both individual and corporate levels. The quality of the student experience should be matched by a quality of staff experience. Assessment of quality is a major feature of university and college life and every UK institution is seeking to improve (or maintain) its score in the various assessment exercises. It is essential that corporate staff development provision and other activities take this into account. For HEFCE assessments, visits are currently the norm, and hence a 'crash' programme of staff development immediately prior to a visit cannot be an acceptable strategy. There is need to both:

● promote to *all* existing staff best practice as appropriate to current audit and assessment parameters;
● implement appropriate training processes for *all* new staff.

For Research Assessment evaluations the position is somewhat different since the emphasis is on key research groups or individuals. There is a need, therefore, to review the research output of entire departments rather than smaller groups. Many institutions implemented a corporate strategy to recruit new staff bringing with them a research portfolio and the immediate potential for publications and other measurable outputs.

There should also be a sustained parallel activity to bring other academic colleagues into the research community and to develop their activities in order that they may be judged equitably against those recruited into institutions in which research resources had originally been made available by the University Grants Committee and other organisations. In the context of research, the objectives will necessarily be long term to take account of the entire process from proposal through to publication.

It is not appropriate to state the rationale for action to promote academic quality merely in institutional terms. It is also essential to consider the matter in respect of the individual academic member of staff, and indeed with reference to the many others whose work makes a significant contribution to the quality of provision. Institutions should seek to ensure that each member of staff is not only motivated to seek excellence in their teaching and research, but *is also provided with appropriate training and development to do so*. Motivation is essential if staff are to operate at the levels of performance now required. The external assessors of teaching or research necessarily evaluate performance by comparison with others. Resource differences are rarely taken into account. The sense of pride in work completed is an essential factor in both teaching and research. In teaching it is the immediate and local knowledge of an individual student's progress and a recognition of the educational added value. In research, a pride in personal abilities is essential if the milestones of published papers and conference presentations are to be attained. Institutions therefore need to develop a substantial and coordinated programme of professional development which is able to:

● focus specifically on the need to promote academic quality (in teaching and research);

- attract support from heads of department, thereby permitting staff release for attendance;
- be attractive to individual members of the academic staff;
- be available over a number of years to enable the programme to gain external credence and hopefully serve as a model for others;
- be subject to the same processes of validation, monitoring, evaluation and review as other programmes.

Viewed from the individual perspective there is a need for the programme to be given accreditation at an appropriate level if the investment in time and effort is to be seen as worthwhile. Several institutions have already addressed this question and provide a coordinated lecturer training programme which leads directly to or may contribute to a validated qualification. As the evaluation of academic quality progresses, and with outside pressure to develop a national, transferable system, it is inevitable that such programmes will become more common. The possession of such a qualification could, of course, become a contributing factor when assessing individuals at recruitment or promotion. Examples of current practice include:

- open-learning based modular programmes (to PG certificate level) in teaching in higher education;
- accredited programmes of lecturer development (teaching skills);
- Masters programmes focusing on action research in teaching and learning;
- modular development programmes for new staff. The initial modules are compulsory for new staff and may be supplemented with optional modules to achieve a Masters level qualification.

The concept is not new to the sector, with many institutions having implemented a variety of compulsory or voluntary models. The existing exemplars of good practice have developed a range of schemes reflecting local requirements. In setting up such a scheme, ie one that takes into account all the stakeholders and locks that activity into the strategic management of the institution, a wide range of factors must be considered, including:

- *Appointments procedures* (ie, to make initial recommendations on the nature, type and level of training and other continuing professional development needed). A similar approach might be adopted at promotion and similar internal interviews. These recommendations could form the basis of an initial appraisal interview conducted as part of the individual's departmental or faculty induction procedures. New academic staff bring with them a range of expertise and experience (from novice teacher through to those with years of experience elsewhere) so it is not desirable to prescribe a single programme. Some new staff will need training as absolute beginners, whereas others will need introductions to the systems, practices and approaches of the institution and perhaps even a weaning away from 'bad habits' acquired elsewhere. In the main, academic staff would participate in a programme focusing on academic quality that pulls together local best practice and adds in appropriate elements from elsewhere.

- *Institutional induction programmes for new academic staff.* Where these exist, they tend to be offered over a couple of days, two or three times a year, or in smaller bites over the first year of appointment. The matter of content must always be the subject of review in order to meet the changing needs of UK higher education in general, and individual institutions and departments in particular. Currently, such programmes should reflect, for example, the six core aspects of HEFCE assessment:

  I. Curriculum design, content and organisation
  II. Teaching, learning and assessment
  III. Student progression and achievement
  IV. Learning resources
  V. Student support and guidance
  VI. Quality assurance and enhancement

- *Mentoring schemes.* For academic staff the scheme could benefit from an increased link with supporting enhanced teaching quality.
- *Peer observation of teaching.* Best practice suggests that peer support schemes flourish where they have an additional, sometimes optional, location within a defined development programme. Again, the strict adherence to informality and confidentiality is an essential ingredient.
- Other appropriate elements of institutional programmes.

Such a scheme should be for *all those with an academic responsibility* (ie, including postgraduates and others as appropriate). New staff should be assigned a mentor on appointment. The role of the individual's personal mentor would be to advise on department-specific aspects of teaching and learning, and possibly to take part in the evaluation of the new lecturer's teaching activities.

Mentors and designated other peers should offer support and guidance to colleagues in their areas of influence. These persons would also be involved in the assessment and evaluation of participants' contributions by providing a local judgement of competence. In essence, this would merely formalise what evidently happens in a number of institutions, often without the knowledge of 'central' staff development and senior management. Typical duration would be two years, and would involve some commitment to attending formal sessions. However, the main thrust of the programme should involve flexible learning and thus be fit 'around' the individual's own curriculum delivery commitments. The main involvement, following best practice in subject development, should be self-directed, with formal face-to-face contact with tutors being kept to a minimum and chiefly concerned with guidance, direction and support.

It was noted earlier that, in its current form, the SEDA scheme may not provide the best 'fit' for some institutions. In particular this applies to evaluating the application of learning and new skills and the impact on the institution and department post-accreditation. That notwithstanding, objectives for programmes should consider those contained within the scheme in the context of the particular needs and priorities of the institution. The modification and adaptation of the objectives for use here does not indicate a preference to actually join the scheme, rather an aversion to reinventing wheels.

Academic staff on the scheme will be expected to demonstrate that they have:

- designed a teaching programme from a course outline, document or syllabus;
- used a wide and appropriate range of teaching and learning methods effectively and efficiently in order to work with large groups, small groups and one-to-one;
- acted professionally in a personal tutor role in a way that is acceptable to a wide range of students;
- used a wide range of assessment techniques to assess student work and to enable students to monitor their own progress;
- used a range of self-, peer and student monitoring and evaluation techniques;
- performed all the teaching support and academic administrative tasks involved in their teaching in their department and their institution;
- developed personal and professional coping strategies within the constraints and opportunities of their institutional setting;
- reflected on their own personal and professional practice and development, assessed their future needs and made a plan for their continuing professional development;
- placed their own teaching practice within the department and faculty experience and requirements.

Research related objectives could include evidence that the participant has:

- designed a research programme and prepared a proposal for funding;
- prepared a research paper in a form suitable for publication in an appropriate journal;
- successfully supervised a postgraduate student to degree completion.

Such a scheme would of course include modules on research and research supervision as well as modules on undergraduate teaching, and would recognise that although the majority of elements will be generic, and thus have applicability across all disciplines, there is need to recognise the specific requirements of the individual faculties and the departments within them. The discipline-specific elements would be determined by subject specialists and would be related to both teaching and research. (Teaching specifics might include reference to, for example, laboratory classes, field trips, practice-based instruction, while research specifics would take account of the different needs of laboratory and library based students.)

Accessibility to all appropriate staff would be essential, with completion of certain modules being a requirement for those taking up additional roles (eg new supervisors of MPhil/PhD students must attend supervisor training sessions – these sessions could provide the basis of a module). Clearly the programme would be offered to in-house staff only, but would be validated and would lead to a postgraduate level qualification (PG diploma, PG certificate or Masters degree as appropriate). The number of modules to be required for a particular named qualification would accord with the institution's normal practice with respect to postgraduate study. The rate of progression would, most appropriately, be flexible although it may be desirable to specify a minimum rate.

The scheme should be largely work-based with assessed activities being competence-based and linked to job related tasks. Assessment of competence would need to be closely related to faculty and departmental principles and practice.

It is essential that such a scheme is flexible, and is not limited to new staff nor always be offered as a complete programme. The current structure of HEFCE and HEQC visits, for example, might trigger participation by some staff teams (perhaps ordering a bespoke package from a published menu). Indeed, the six core aspects to be assessed by HEFCE could be adopted as module titles, as is the case on a number of projects and programmes in English institutions.

5. Consider the position of the individual member of staff

A method of agreeing and recording objectives actions and outcomes is an essential component in effective delivery and evaluation. As an outcome, and in support of, the appraisal process or training and development reviews, staff can draw up a

Purpose	Objectives	Methodology	Action from	Reviewed by
To be able to chair team meetings	To develop 'facilitation' skills: – listening skills; – controlling the meeting; – summarising skills.	1. Attendance on chairing meetings course. 2. Shadow experienced colleague at Academic Standards Committee 3. Observation of team meeting and feedback by manager	January February March	February End February End March
To create more time to 'supervise' the team	To develop time management systems To identify tasks that can be delegated To develop planning skills	1. Attend time management module 2. Coaching from manager/mentor	April Mid-May	Early May End June
To improve written reports so that report writing can be delegated by manager	To be able to write in an appropriate style	1. Coaching and feedback from manager 2. Review colleagues' reports for style and presentation	Immediately	Mid-May

Figure 13.3: *A personal development plan*

personal development plan. There is a range of formats for these plans, but basically they comprise documentation highlighting agreed actions. They can be very elaborate or (preferably) kept very simple. At their simplest they would include:

- the purpose of the training or development action(s);
- the objectives of the action(s);
- the methodology to be used to meet the action(s);
- the date the action(s) should be started by;
- the date the outcome from the action(s) should be reviewed by, ie were objectives met?

Ideally the plans should include long-term, medium-term and short-term objectives, but this may vary depending on the complexity of the individual's role. Figure 13.3 illustrates this by looking at a head of department who needs to develop skills in chairing meetings.

6. Consider the evaluation of those areas that fall outside professional accreditation

For other professional staff working in higher education there are various nationally recognised and transferable professional qualifications for entry into their profession and often for progression within it. Evaluation of the individual's development in the professional sense is therefore subject in some degree to the type and level of scrutiny argued for in 4 above. Should some variation on 4 above be adopted by an institution, the remaining gap in the evaluation process with regard to all staff would be those areas that fall outside the remit of such programmes. All staff participate in a variety of training and development activities that are in support of, or complementary to, their role. Examples include appraisal training, stress management, assertion training, various in-house management development programmes and the ubiquitous IT training and development activities. With regard to IT and management development programmes – often a key objectives in institutional, team and development plans – Dearing notes that:

> 'Academics are all committed to keeping abreast of the latest research and ideas in their discipline, but few of them have the opportunity to keep at the forefront of developments in how to teach their subject. According to our survey of staff in higher education (Report 3), only just over half of academics have ever received any training in how to teach and over two thirds of those had received training only at the beginning of their careers. This inevitably means that a large proportion have had no training in, for example, the use of information technology for learning and teaching. Likewise, although many academic staff have significant management responsibilities – for example the financial and personnel responsibilities of a head of department – they rarely have the training to support these functions.'
>
> NCIHE Report (1997) Chapter 3, Higher Education Today, 3.40

If institutional objectives are clear, the appraisal process works and the various measures employed by the institution with regard to quality assurance and enhancement are informing the planning process, then all training and development actions relate to clear institutional, departmental and individual needs. Appropriate instruments can be used to measure reaction, learning, application of learning, the impact on the department/institution and return on investment as appropriate. This, however, should be done through *existing* systems. All programmes can be treated as modules and subject to the same quality assurance processes as 'normal' modules. Indeed, the various 'modules' of an agreed development programme for an individual could count towards an accredited qualification, in-house or otherwise. Following up post-accreditation would be via 'normal' routes such as appraisal, peer review, observation, mentoring, coaching. Reporting structures are therefore the same for all programmes of study be they short or long, for staff (as students) or students. In other words, the whole institution has a learning agenda, given that it has an agreed commonality of purpose. The stereotype of the isolated staff developer armed only with the data on how many people attended centrally run programmes should become a thing of the past. Staff development could then move increasingly towards seeing itself as a collection of interrelated projects drawn from, and informing, institutional and departmental plans and supported by, and supporting, appraisal and review processes.

A final comment

All of us in higher education are all working towards the same goals, ie to:

- plan, undertake, support and disseminate research, scholarship and related activities;
- design, implement, support and evaluate learning and teaching;
- develop and review strategy, and lead, manage and administer systems and services in support of academic practice (UCoSDA, 1996).

In essence, this is the enhancing of the quality of the student experience and the expanding and extending of the field of human knowledge and understanding, whether we are directly involved in teaching and research or seemingly far removed from it in maintenance or security. Effective evaluation can only tell us whether what we have done individually and collectively has been worth doing if we have agreed what it is we intend to do and what the best means of getting there are.

There are clear messages for all stakeholders in UK higher education, but perhaps especially for those charged with its management. I leave the last words to Lao Tse:

'The teacher is best when people barely know he exists

Not so good when people obey and acclaim him

Worse when they despise him.

"Fail to honour people, they fail to honour you."

But of a good leader, who talks little,

When his work is done, his aim fulfilled, they will say:

"We did this ourselves".'

Extracts from: Continuing Professional Development (CPD) of Staff in Higher Education (HE): Informing Strategic Thinking UK UCoSDA Task Force Five (July, 1994)

The dotted lines indicate where text has been omitted.

1. Introduction – why provide CPD for all staff in HE?

(a) Change in higher education (HE) and its implications

Higher education institutions (HEIs) have been and are a focus of radical and rapid changes. The sources of influence for these changes are numerous and varied: political, social, economic, educational, epistemological, legal, technological. The results are that those engaging in the provision of higher education have had to:

- respond to more diverse educational needs and steadily increasing expectations;
- be more accountable about their performance through quality assessment and audit of educational provision, research assessment, and media analyses and investigations.
- respond to these accountability measures by improving the quality of their research, teaching, consultancy activities and other institutional services;

The increasingly diverse educational needs of the adult (post-18) population in preparation for the changing nature of employment and career development is leading to greater differentiation of missions, goals and activities across the expanded higher education system. In sum, there has been a dramatic shift in the climate within which universities and colleges operate which has contributed to significant changes within the culture of individual organisations. (1)

(b) Demonstration rather than assumption of excellence

A central aim of UK universities and colleges has been and continues to be the pursuit of excellence in their individually targeted areas of activity. Until the late 1980s only partial and uncoordinated evidence had been expected from HEIs to indicate that they were achieving the excellence they sought:

- In research: bidding systems of varying degrees of rigour had existed for the procurement of funding from a variety of public, private and charitable bodies. The results of projects so funded were equally variably evaluated; a peer review system formed the basis of the evaluation of publications.
- In learning, teaching and curriculum design: the curricula and methods of teaching in vocational subject areas were subject to the scrutiny of professional accrediting bodies or government departments (eg Education by DFE); the design, monitoring and review of courses and their teaching in the then poly-technics were evaluated and approved by the former Council for National Academic Awards (CNAA); certificate and diploma courses were accredited by a variety of national bodies according to variable procedures.

These examples illustrate the lack of coherence in the previous procedures for assuring the quality of research and educational practices in HEIs.

Since 1990 change in this area has been radical and swift. The Funding Councils' cyclical research assessment exercises, the quality assessment procedures for evaluating educational provision in subject areas, the work of the Higher Education Quality Council together with the continuing accreditation activities of the bodies alluded to above, now combine to form a more systematic, but arguably not yet coherent approach to the assurance of the quality of academic practice. Moreover, the fact that these new systems do in some cases, eg research assessment and quality assessment of educational provision in Scotland, inform funding allocations, and will increasingly do so, sharpens their impact on institutional policies and practices. In summary, all the core activity of higher education institutions is now subject to continuing external scrutiny; the achievement of excellence or even competence will no longer be assumed, but must be demonstrated.

(c) The role of staff in institutional development

It is well recognised by universities and colleges that their greatest cost – usually in excess of 70% of overall expenditure – is that of their staff. However, this recognition is not always translated into an appreciation of the value of that human resource and the need continuously to maintain and enhance its potential. It is of benefit to any organisation to have professional standards in place for the recruitment, selection, monitoring and promotion of all staff as well as to train and develop all of them continuously to the highest level. If the staff are of high quality and have embraced the concept of life-long learning, they are more likely to have positive attitudes towards change and to be responsive and flexible to the changing demands made of them.

In this paper we emphasise the importance of ensuring CPD provision for all staff across an institution for three principal reasons:

- New developments in organisations are most effectively implemented when all staff involved are properly inducted into their significance, implications and operations.

  For example, developments such as the introduction of the Higher Education Charters have implications for the way in which all staff – Heads of Department, lecturers, technicians, secretaries – view and work with students and other consumers. All staff require knowledge and training to respond effectively to such new developments.

- The changes referred to in the preceding sections increasingly require groups of staff drawn from a variety of staff categories to work together in the provision of teaching and the development of research.

  For example, curricula developments such as modularisation and consequent new learning, teaching and assessment methods, require an integrated staff approach to provision, with a variety of staff – lecturers, librarians, technicians, technologists and secretaries – working as a team of 'learning managers'.

- New initiatives such as the research assessment exercise, the educational quality assessments and the proposals in the White Paper (1993) on research 'Realising our Potential', all require a higher level of 'professionalism' of staff.

  For example, the Funding Councils' quality assessments of the educational provision of subject areas require two 'professionalisms' of academics: that they be both (a) professionals in their subject, ie as engineers, doctors, architects, artists, critics, etc, and (b) professional teachers, ie trained in the skills for that particular area of their responsibilities. Secondly, the research White Paper alludes to a need for the proper management of research and to skills training which might develop that. Such training might not only involve the researchers, but also, for example, technicians with financial responsibilities in the project.

The preceding examples illustrate both the need for a system of continuing professional development for all staff, and specifically areas in which CPD can better prepare staff for their roles and responsibilities, thereby enabling the institution and its faculties to achieve the goals they set and the excellence they pursue.

(d) The language of this paper

Hitherto the concepts of continuing professional development (CPD) and life-long learning have been used without explanation. Both require and deserve more detailed analysis. CPD is a term we use here for the following reasons:

- The term and concept has currency in many organisations. It is increasingly used with reference to all staff and, in many cases, in relationship with cyclical appraisal schemes and personal development plans which operate and are defined in conjunction with departmental and institutional goals. One of the major concerns of this paper is the encouragement of the integration of such activities into the strategic planning of the institution.

- The word 'development' is a broader concept than, for example, 'training' and implies a longer term approach and one which has benefits for the individual as well as the organisation. 'Training' has a more task-specific focus and an unfortunate connotation of remedial activity, ie to bring someone up to a standard of competence rather than support them in going beyond that.

- The term 'professional' is more sensitive and contentious. The arguments for and against the notion of, for example, an academic as a professional are numerous and complex and have been rehearsed elsewhere (Piper, 1993; Kogan and Moses, 1994.) Some readers might believe that the word 'professional' only applies to some groups of staff in universities, for example those in the academic and related categories. The Task Force members would argue that the term is increasingly in more widespread use and applies to all staff in HE. It is used in this paper with reference to all staff, and is particularly selected to emphasise the need for the development of a professional approach to all tasks which support our core activities of learning, research and teaching.

- Finally the notion of 'continuation' is of critical importance. Just as strategic planning is a regular, continuing process, so also is one of its integral component parts – the continuing planning for the use and work of staff, and for their development to undertake that work most effectively.

Other terms which might have been used – such as 'staff development' or 'staff training' – would have omitted one or other of the elements outlined above. We do, however, recognise that preferences are strongly perceived for particular terminology and we acknowledge here the sensitivities. We hope that readers' personal preferences – perhaps slightly different from our own – will not inhibit their appreciation of the ideas put forward.

Reference has been made to 'life-long learning'. In current times (and inevitably for the future) it is important to recruit and appoint individual staff not only with the knowledge, skills and attitudes required now for the particular post, but also with the capacities to be flexible, adaptable, creative and amenable to change. In other words, with the capability of learning continuously throughout his or her career. Moreover, to attract and retain such individuals, institutions and their faculties need to develop into 'learning organisations'. Briefly, a 'learning organisation' is one (a) in which a culture is created by its leaders and managers, which fosters continuing learning and development for all staff, (b) in which these processes are directly related to the achievement of its aims and goals, and (c) which provides adequate levels of resourcing – both time and money – for such continuing development to take place. Further features can be explored in Lessem (1991) and Marquardt and Reynolds (1994).

For both individuals and institutions in higher education such developments as (a) diversification of funding sources and devolution of managerial responsibility for finances, (b) technological innovations, and (c) changes in the nature of the curriculum and the relationship between learner and tutor, all combine to make the adoption of the concept of life-long learning a necessity. Without continuing learning and development individuals and groups are unlikely to succeed. Without becoming a 'learning organisation', an institution is likely to become dysfunctional to the extent that its effectiveness, credibility and perhaps existence become questionable. One of the main challenges facing UK universities and colleges is that of changing organisations which are essentially about and for learning into explicitly conscious and functioning learning organisations.

(e) The structure of and issues in this paper

In order to support institutions in responding to the challenges presented in this introduction, the areas explored further in this paper are:

- approaches to CPD in a variety of organisations; national frameworks for future development: Investors in People, NVQs and National Education and Training Targets;
- policies and structures for effective and strategic CPD in higher education;
- the need for mission-related CPD for all staff and the consequent diversity of models and methods needed across different HEIs;
- tensions which arise in establishing CPD; gaining the commitment of individual staff, various staff groups, campus unions, etc, and balancing benefits to individuals and to the institution;
- resourcing levels for organisation-wide CPD, and establishing the benefits of the investment of resources;
- accreditation routes and qualifications; issues of portability and transferability;
- current changes in the provision of CPD within institutions of HE.

These aspects and issues are considered in four main sections:

- CPD in organisations outside the HE sector;
- CPD within HE;
- current issues in the provision of CPD within HE;
- implementing continuing and coherent professional development.

These sections are supplemented by case studies in the appendices to the text. Finally a series of twelve key recommendations is proposed for consideration by strategic leaders in and for higher education and by colleagues who are responsible for the planning, organisation, delivery and monitoring of development and training for all staff groups.

2. Continuing professional development in organisations outside higher education

(f) Implications for higher education institutions

(i)   since the mid-1980s there has been a dramatically increased awareness of the importance of the development and training of staff on the part of government, the public and private sectors, and professional bodies;

(ii) this has led a wide range of organisations to commit themselves to making systematic provision for staff training and development before entry to employment, during the initial learning phase, and thereafter on a continuing basis;

(iii) in making such provision, organisations have found it helpful to link their business objectives and staff development and training needs, and to produce a strategic plan for the latter, this being a requirement for organisations seeking 'Investors in People' status and part of the recommended Code of Practice of The Engineering Council;

(iv) to put such plans into operation and ensure a two-way flow between institutional objectives and individual needs, organisations have made staff training and development a specific responsibility of line managers;

(v)   in all the cases covered, the primary instrument for articulating needs, identifying appropriate training and development opportunities, evaluating these, and monitoring progress, has been a personal development plan/file for every employee;

(vi) organisations have, where appropriate, been prepared to resource adequately staff development and training through in-house/external provision, open learning centres, paid study time or study leave, help with fees, etc.

Some implications for higher education institutions are that:

(a) if they are not to fall behind other organisations and possibly jeopardise recruitment and retention of their staff, they need to pay more attention to the development and training of all staff and commit themselves to the introduction of appropriate systems;

(b) the starting point should be to articulate staff development and training needs within the light of organisational aims and objectives and produce an appropriate strategy covering all staff in the institution;

(c) responsibility for implementing this should be shared by senior management, line management and the employee, and should formally rest with line managers within institutions;

(d) personal development plans should be introduced for all categories of staff;

(e) resources should be made available for all staff to undertake development and training activities which correspond to identified needs and contribute to the achievement of organisational aims and objectives.

There are some institutions in higher education which have already addressed some or all of these points, and examples are discussed in the next section.

3. CPD for staff in universities and colleges

(a) Background

The traditional approach to the training and development of staff in HEIs has been (and still continues in some institutions to be) biased heavily in favour of provision for academic staff; predominantly departmentally based and discipline/research-related; largely uncoordinated and unsystematic with little monitoring and accountability; with inadequate resource available for professional preparation for functions other than research, ie for teaching and for administration and management. There has been comparatively little resource available for academic-related and administrative staff, and even less for other ancillary and allied staff such as secretaries and technicians. The impact of the changing environment of higher education on strategic thinking and policy making has brought with it a recognisable pattern of innovation and modification to systems and structures for staff's professional development in many universities and colleges. The diversity of mission across the sector means that different institutions have different patterns of need in this context, as in other policy areas. It is clear nevertheless that many universities are introducing new programmes for the professional development of their staff which are more integrated, more accessible and more flexible. It must also be recognised that much of this development has been of recent date and many of the most interesting initiatives in this area still remain to be evaluated.

The marked trend which has been discernible over the past five years, is a movement towards continuing professional development schemes which are a part of an organisation-wide, more centrally directed policy. A range of different influences and developments, some external and some internal underlie this shift in policy and practice. Universities are increasingly seeing the professional development of their staff as a key part of strategic planning. As such it is inextricably linked to their plans for quality assurance and quality enhancement, and viewed as supporting the attainment of strategic objectives, and as contributing to the greater efficiency and effectiveness of the organisation. For all these reasons, a dynamic and rapidly changing picture of continuing professional development in universities emerges from any survey of work currently being undertaken.

... it can be seen that (a) more opportunities for all staff groups exist now than ever before and (b) that all HEIs have some provision and a designated coordinator in place. In no HEI, however, could it be confidently asserted that there exists a system of comprehensive, coherent, career-long CPD which embraces all staff at all levels and which is integrated into the institution's strategic objectives. The issues put forward in the following section are ones which need to be addressed if such systems are to be developed within HEIs.

4. Current issues in the provision of CPD within HE

The questions and issues raised by the preceding section in respect of CPD provision current and future in HE are now examined briefly in four sub-sections:

- strategies, responsibilities and resources;
- access and equitability;
- accreditation, portability and diversity;
- benefits and evaluation.

(d) Benefits and evaluation

One of the most critical questions increasingly often asked of CPD planners and providers is why this investment should be made and what the benefits are. They are hard questions to answer, since it is difficult (a) to identify clearly the reasons for, eg better performance, enhanced skills, increased knowledge, heightened job satisfaction and motivation and (b) to isolate definitively staff development and training as key reasons. Examples in external organisations, such as those illustrated in Section 2 of this report suggest that this investment pays off. It is argued, by representatives of The Rover Group, that their policy and practice of extensive CPD has been a key contributory factor in their achievement of recent success. Reports on training in Britain over the past decade have linked the relative economic success of competitor nations such as Germany, Japan and the USA to their larger average investment in continuing professional and vocational development. Such anecdotal evidence may, however, not always be sufficiently convincing. The Task Force recognises the need within HE to concentrate on the evaluation of CPD and its associated benefits, and (a) recommends further development work in this area and (b) offers the brief article in Appendix 5 as an illustration of how such evaluation and calculation of benefits might be undertaken. The group is well aware that the most precious and stretched resource of all staff in HE is time, and acknowledges the need to substantiate current anecdotal evidence of benefits, in order to underpin the central role of CPD.

5. Implementing continuing and coherent CPD for all staff

(a) Altering perceptions of and structures for continuing CPD

Perceptions of CPD
If perceptions of the role of continuing professional development are to develop towards the acknowledgement of its critical place in supporting the management of change, it will require that managers at all levels include planning for training and development within their strategic planning exercises at every stage – annual, triennial and/or quinquennial plans. It will require resources – staff time, facilities, materials, equipment as well as finance – to be committed to the achievement of those staff development plans at departmental and institutional levels. A coherent infrastructure for continuing training and development will need to be created, which will include policy formation, strategic planning, adequately resourced provision and continuing monitoring and evaluation of the function. In short, a culture needs to be developed across the institution which is supportive of the notions of life-long learning and of continuing investment in the most valuable resource the organisation has – its people. Leaders and managers must play the major part in the development of that culture, but must do this through full and sensitive consultation with all involved parties, in order that agreement is gained and commitment achieved for a corporate framework.

Structures for professional development
Current structures for providing CPD derive in part from historical developments and from present external pressures. Their diversity reflects the transitional state they are in as well as lack of clarity within the higher education community of the function they support. It is worth exploring a range of models (not definitive) which exists, in order to identify key issues for consideration in the organisation of staff development.

6. Twelve recommendations for strategic CPD in higher education

In the evolution, policies, models, structures and processes explored in this paper, an attempt has been made both to define professional development for staff as it exists currently in higher education and to extract from the definition issues which, when considered, might lead to future improvements in provision. Two words often most obviously lacking in the examination and analysis of current continuing professional development are 'policy' and 'strategy'. This is because most staff developers find that their situation obliges them to work at the tactical and operational levels only. Herein lies the basis for the ways forward, if CPD is to be enabled to play its full and valuable part in enriching the individuals' and the institution's activities, and in contributing to the achievement of goals in each case. At the present time the operations and tactics of those responsible for CPD are in many cases supplemented by 'paper policies'. The missing link is strategy. In order to achieve strategic continuing professional development the following actions are recommended for consideration within institutions:

1. Institutional and departmental review and strategic planning should incorporate at all stages strategic planning for CPD for all staff, informed by the specialists in CPD.

2. There needs to be encouragement from leaders and managers towards greater recognition across the institution of the value of CPD for staff and of its contribution to the achievement of goals.

3. The resourcing of staff development and CPD provision needs to be reviewed in all respects, ie the financial allocations, the staffing levels, the quality of the staff, the time and space allocated to the function, etc. Such a review should particularly lead to greater parity of provision of CPD across all the staff groups in HEIs.

4. The locus of the institution-wide staff development facility and the various nodes of responsibility for CPD provision need continually to be reviewed within the context (a) of the particular institution and its mission and goals, and (b) of the changing external environment.

5. Some form of reorganisation may need to be considered of those central services which have a remit for or a relationship to staff development, in order to enhance its strategic position and role.

6. Clearer planning and guidance is needed across and within HEIs for an effective, integrated relationship to be made between staff appraisal and the provision of CPD.

7. There needs to be greater understanding – most particularly at departmental/school level – of all the related and relative responsibilities for CPD planning and provision.

8. The role of departmentally-focused staff development activity needs to be explored more fully, particularly in the light of the research assessment exercise and the quality assessment of educational provision, both of which focus on particular subject areas.

9. A study needs to be funded and undertaken at system-wide level of the benefits of investment in CPD and of the related costs. Cost-benefit analysis in this field is complex, but data need to be gathered and analysed which might (a) give greater clarity of current investment within and across HEIs and of the benefits derived, and (b) encourage greater commitment to the activity.

10. A further system-wide survey and analysis should be funded of appropriate accreditation routes and qualifications for CPD for the various staff in higher

education. Such a study should (a) take account of the increasing demand for portable qualifications, but (b) should focus on the special needs of higher education and on the increasing diversity of institutional missions and consequent need for alternative routes.

11. Greater collaboration needs to be fostered across universities and colleges in the consideration, planning and provision of CPD for their staffs, in order to provide more efficiently for the needs. Such extended networking and cooperation could be built upon the existing structures and their work, such as: the Midlands M1/M69 network and other regional groupings; the Committee of Scottish Higher Education Principals (COSHEP) Staff Development Committee and its sub-groups focused on specific CPD functions; the Higher Education Quality Council and particularly its Quality Enhancement Group; the Staff and Educational Development Association (SEDA); and the Universities' and Colleges' Staff Development Agency (UCoSDA).

12. In summary of the preceding recommendations, institutions and cross-institutional groupings and agencies should support action in all these areas, in order that HEIs may develop as 'learning organisations', which will in turn enhance their own credibility as providers of and for learning.

UCoSDA, 1994

Evaluation of Training and Development Effectiveness

Name...

Section/Department...

Part A Prior to the training or development action

1. Proposed training/development activity: ...

2. Details, eg dates, locations, cost, etc

3. The institutional objective the proposed activity will help to achieve

4. What skills and/or knowledge will be learnt as a result of the activity

5. How will the new skills and/or knowledge be applied after the activity

6. Line manager's comments, ie expectations in terms of targets or standards

Signatures... participant   .... date

.... Line Manager .... date

Part B Immediately after the training and/or developmental activity

1. Did the participant attend yes/no (if no give reason)

2. To what extent has this activity met the agreed training and/or developmental need

   Please circle   Not at all 1 2 3 4 Totally

   Comments

3. How will the learning be applied?

4. What help/support is needed to put the learning into practice

5. To what extent did the activity represent:

    Value for money (or other agreed measure)

    Please circle   Not at all 1 2 3 4 Totally

    An acceptable standard of delivery

    Please circle   Not at all 1 2 3 4 Totally

    Comments

6. Agreed date to review...

Signatures.. participant   .... date

    .... Line Manager .... date

Part C Review to monitor impact on performance

1. How has the learning been applied since the activity?

2. To what extent have the agreed objectives/targets or standards been met

    Please circle   Not at all 1 2 3 4 Totally

    Comments

3. If learning has not been applied please state why

4. What further action or review is required?

Signatures... participant   .... date

           .... Line Manager .... date

The National Standard for Effective Investment in People

---

1. Principle One: Commitment

An Investor in People makes a commitment from the top to develop all employees to achieve its business objectives.

1.1 The commitment from top management to train and develop employees is communicated effectively throughout the organisation

1.2 Employees at all levels are aware of the broad aims or vision of the organisation

1.3 The employer has considered what employees at all levels will contribute to the success of the organisation, and has communicated this effectively to them

1.4 Where representative structures exist, communication takes place between management and representatives on the vision of where the organisation is going and the contribution that employees (and their representatives) will make to its success

2. Principle Two: Planning

An Investor in People regularly reviews the needs and plans the training and development of all employees.

2.1 A written but flexible plan sets out the organisation's goals and targets

2.2 A written plan identifies the organisation's training and development needs, and specifies what action will be taken to meet these needs

2.3 Training and development needs are regularly reviewed against goals and targets at the organisation, team and individual level

2.4 A written plan identifies the resources that will be used to meet training and development needs

2.5 Responsibility for training and developing employees is clearly identified and understood throughout the organisation, starting at the top

2.6 Objectives are set for training and development actions at the organisation, team and individual level

2.7 Where appropriate, training and development needs are linked to external standards such as National Vocational Qualifications (NVQs) or Scottish Vocational Qualifications (SVQs) and units

3. Principle Three: Action

An Investor in People takes action to train and develop individuals on recruitment and throughout their employment.

3.1 All new employees are introduced effectively to the organisation and all employees new to a job are given the training and development they need to do that job

3.2 Managers are effective in carrying out their responsibilities for training and developing employees

3.3 Managers are actively involved in supporting employees to meet their training and development needs.

3.4 All employees are made aware of the training and development opportunities open to them

3.5 All employees are encouraged to help identify and meet their job related training and development needs

3.6 Action takes place to meet the training and development needs of individuals, teams and the organisation

4. Principle Four: Evaluation

An Investor in People evaluates the investment in training and development to assess achievement and improve future effectiveness.

4.1 The organisation evaluates the impact of training and development actions on knowledge, skills and attitude

4.2 The organisation evaluates the impact of training and development actions on performance

4.3 The organisation evaluates the contribution of training and development to the achievement of its goals and targets

4.4 Top management understands the broad costs and benefits of training and developing employees

4.5 Action takes place to implement improvements to training and development identified as a result of evaluation

4.6 Top management's continuing commitment to training and developing employees is demonstrated to all employees

The University of the West of England Evaluating Training and Development – Appraisal Skills

---

1. Background

In 1993/4 the University set up a Working Group to develop an appraisal and development scheme for support staff. As part of its objectives the Group were to recommend mechanisms for implementing the recommended scheme and a proposed training programme to support implementation.

The organisation had in the previous year committed to appraisal as a concept and had developed an appraisal scheme for academic staff. The reasons for introducing appraisal were varied and related to the following:

- government policy to increase accountability via quality audit and assessment;
- the desire to introduce 'performance management' as a concept to the university, ie to require managers to more effectively manage poor performance as well as develop good performers and hence maximise employee potential;
- to introduce a mechanism for analysing training needs on an organisational scale;
- to involve staff in the change management process and related issues;
- to give all staff equal access to development opportunities.

The Group agreed that the proposed scheme should be piloted amongst a random group of staff and the training programme would also, therefore, be a 'pilot'.

2. Objectives

The training objectives were agreed as follows. Participants should:

- develop their knowledge and understanding of the university scheme and understand the rationale behind introducing appraisal into the university;
- develop an understanding of the skills and approach required to conduct successful appraisal interviews;

- identify the skills and techniques to deal with challenging situations in appraisal interviews;
- practise appraisal interview skills and techniques.

3. Programme delivery

It was agreed by the Working Group that an external consultant with experience of appraisal training should deliver the programme. It was agreed that this should ideally also be someone who had some knowledge of the university.

Training had previously been provided for academic staff when an academic appraisal scheme had been introduced in 1993. The possibility of employing the same consultants for implementation of the support staff programme was therefore considered as an option. Thought was given to:

- the feedback from previous course participants;
- the daily cost;
- the relationship that had been established already;
- the potential audience.

A review of these factors led to the conclusion that an alternative consultant would be approached.

4. Length of the programme

Appraisal skills training for academic staff had been one day in length. Discussions with the consultant chosen to lead the 'pilot' training programme concluded that a one-day programme, although tight, would allow adequate time to cover all essential elements.

The Group were also mindful of the fact that the training was to be compulsory and, because of other time pressures managers were under, the training would need to be condensed into the minimum time scale possible.

5. Content of the pilot programme

I met on several occasions with the trainer that had been identified to determine the content of the day-long programme. The programme then comprised:

- a brief overview of the appraisal scheme;
- discussion and practical exercises around key skill areas, eg communicating, listening, etc;
- role plays – the content of these was intended to reflect some possible situations that an appraiser might have to handle in the university.

This course was to be run for two groups of appraisers. These were people who had been part of the Working Group as well as potential appraisers within Personnel Services.

6. Evaluation of the pilot programme

Evaluation criteria were drawn up based on the objectives set, which included:

- Did the programme develop your understanding of the scheme?
- Was the content relevant to your role as an appraiser?
- Was there adequate opportunity for you to practise your skills?
- What was your view of the length of the programme?
- Was the course leader able to meet the objectives?

Evaluation of each event took place at the end of the day. This was done by means of a group discussion based on the above. The results were fed back to the course leader at the end of the first event so that the course could be updated based on the changes recommended.

6.1 Conclusion

The outcome of the two day-long events was as follows:

- too much time was spent discussing the operation of the scheme and this did not leave enough time for the real 'skills' training to be covered effectively. The course leader was considered not to have managed the group discussion effectively;
- the practical exercises, such as those on body language and listening, were not wholly effective;
- the role plays were useful in that they related to scenarios in the university and should be retained, but needed to be adjusted;
- there was not enough time to cover the content in sufficient depth.

6.2 Outcomes

- There should be a specific briefing about the appraisal scheme included in the programme, but separate from the skills training. This would allow time for questions to be asked about the scheme and would present an opportunity for discussion about the value of appraisal. This would also potentially avoid the skills training being taken over by discussion about the value (or otherwise) of appraisal.
- Appraisal skills training cannot effectively take place over one day. The course would therefore be extended to at least a day and a half.
- Given the importance of the training as the mechanism by which appraisal was

being introduced into the university, the Group concluded that the consultant did not have all of the skills required in this critical area.

- Course numbers would be restricted on each programme.
- The programme would take place off site, partly to ensure that adequate facilities were available and also to confirm the importance of appraisal to all staff.
- Training of appraisers was not sufficient alone as the scheme was new to all staff. Briefing sessions would therefore be made available to all appraisees.

7. Revised training programme

7.1 The first issue was to identify a possible trainer. Interviews were held with a number of people. (The consultants came via recommendation from other universities and/or colleagues.)

A conclusion was reached as to who could provide the most effective programme based on their previous experience, interest in the subject, suggestions about the programme content, their 'fit' within the organisation and the working relationship.

7.2 A two-day programme was drawn up comprising a half-day briefing led by Personnel Services staff followed by a one-and-a-half day skills training course. The programme took place off site.

The content followed much of the previous format, but could be developed more thoroughly, and specific time was spent on the role play exercises. Participants were also asked to prepare for the role plays by bringing information with them to the course. In this way it was made more meaningful for each individual attending.

8. Evaluation of the revised programme

8.1 The post-course evaluation questionnaires are used as a mechanism for assessing immediate reaction to the event. In the early stages immediately on completion of the course these were discussed by the trainer and the Personnel Manager. Suggestions for changes to the programme could then be discussed and agreed quickly and changes were introduced into the next course. (This was important given the number of courses that were taking place over a relatively limited period.)

Verbal comment was also sought from participants in addition to the questionnaire. This was initially obtained at the end of the course (without the course leader being present). Alternatively, views were obtained via the telephone.

8.2 Further comments received from delegates and their managers indicate that some staff would value a 'refresher' course, and this will be developed.

8.3 Post-course evaluation of the training has been very positive. The course itself is well received despite the fact that participants have to spend two days away from their job, which is something that they are concerned about when booking a place. All indications are that they consider the two days to have been time well spent.

8.4 The appraiser briefing sessions have generally been positively received. Comments are made via post-course evaluation, but also the need for questions to be raised about the operation of the scheme during the skills training has been significantly reduced.

Conclusion

I think that it is fair to say that we have now developed a quality training programme which meets its objectives as stated above. A large part of this is due to the commitment and enthusiasm of the trainer who has an in-depth subject knowledge, but who has also been able to convince all but a few managers of the value of the appraisal process.

The other important point to note is that this type of programme cannot be developed overnight. The trainer has made many changes in order to refine the programme by taking on board the comments/criticisms made, and at the same time her knowledge of the organisation and the specific scheme has grown over time.

9. Evaluation at an organisational level

9.1 An evaluation in 1996 of the appraisal scheme itself found that it has been implemented in all areas and is considered to have 'added value', although it would be difficult to assess this in cost/benefit terms. This review has also led to the conclusion that the appraisal cycle should be moved to a two-year cycle.

9.2 The scheme has an appeals procedure which enables staff to pursue issues when they consider that their appraisal has been handled inappropriately. The appeals process is via Personnel. At this stage no appeals have reached us. Although there are no doubt disagreements occurring between appraiser and appraisee as part of the process, none of them has become sufficiently serious to warrant Personnel involvement. One can therefore assume that appraisers are, for the most part, applying what they have learnt from the appraisal skills programme.

9.3 Managers appear to be more actively managing performance of their staff. This may not be as a direct result of appraisal, of course, but the process, if done properly, does require there to be a review and discussion of strengths and weaknesses and an action plan to pursue these (although the process is specifically separate from the discipline procedure).

9.4 More disappointing, perhaps, has been the information appraisal has produced about training needs of the organisation as a whole. Information from appraisers about development needs has tended to be still relatively fragmented. However, I think it is fair to say that the general interest in having access to appropriate development activities has increased. This aspect will be reviewed and changes may be made to the documentation as a result.

Summary

The provision of an effective training programme has been critical to the successful implementation of the appraisal scheme. At an individual level feedback has been positive immediately following attendance at the course. Subsequent meetings with managers and staff have demonstrated that the training has been transferred to the workplace. Indeed, some staff who approached the training and the process with great scepticism have felt very positive about the process as a result of attending the course.

A specific cost benefit analysis is not feasible. However, the scheme underpinned by the training does better equip managers to learn and change into the future. For many of them this was the first time that they have attended 'management' skills training on a compulsory basis. Given that appraisal skills can be used in many more scenarios than just an appraisal interview this is a very positive step forward for the individuals and the organisation as a whole.

Pam Fitsimmons
Training and Development, Personnel Manager,
University of the West of England

University of Northumbria at Newcastle Post-course Telephone Questionnaire

---

Hello, my name is … , I'm calling from Staff Development. We are conducting a survey to evaluate the success of the recent pilot of one-to-one training delivered by staff within Information Services. I wonder if you could spare a few moments to answer some brief questions about the one-to-one training you received?

Please answer yes or no to the following questions

1. Has receiving the training had an impact on your everyday work?

IF NOT WHY NOT?
    a) Have you been able to set up any new systems in your section as a result of receiving the training?
    b) Can you carry out tasks more efficiently?
2. Have you made any improvements to current systems since receiving the training?
3. Have you referred to the Plain English Guide/found it useful since receiving the training?
4. Have you noticed an improvement in the quality of the work you produce?
5. Have you noticed an increase in the speed with which you produce your work?
6. Have you noticed an increase in the volume of work you process using your PC?
7. Do you feel generally more confident operating your PC?
8. Since receiving the training, have you been able to help/solve problems for other staff in your section?
9. Do you think you are now capable of progressing further yourself (ie, without the help of further training)?
10. Would you find self-help materials a useful method of further learning (books, videos, CBT packages etc)?

University of Hertfordshire
Draft Staff Development Policy

A: Policy and strategic aims

Commitment and strategic aims

The University believes that its success is ultimately dependent upon the efforts and quality of its staff. It sees the capability and commitment of its staff, at all levels and in all roles, as essential to the achievement of its Mission and goals. The University recognises that it must make provision for the work-related and personal career development of its staff.

The University, through its Faculties, Centres and Departments, therefore undertakes to plan and provide a comprehensive and strategically-led staff development service for all its staff and functions, delivered on an equitable basis. This service will:

- respond to staff development needs, as diagnosed by individuals and their managers, and by leaders of University functions;
- support new staff in their induction to the University;
- facilitate the development of life-long learning in all staff;
- be proactive in planning and support to anticipate change;
- organise, promote and maintain a wide variety of activities to help staff to take stock, update and extend their knowledge, skills and capabilities;
- encourage the dissemination of good practice in all areas through staff development activity;
- monitor and evaluate staff development activity so as to continually learn and improve provision.

As evidence of its general commitment to its staff, the University has also made a specific commitment to the Investors in People national initiative.

Definition

Staff development includes everything that is done by and for staff in order to maintain and extend their work-related knowledge, skills and capabilities.

APPENDIX 6

Purpose

The purpose of this *policy statement* is to ensure a common understanding as to the aims and principles of staff development within the University.

The purpose of *staff development* is seen by the University as having two interrelated main strands:

i) to encourage and support all staff to achieve individual work and career goals;
ii) to enable and assist all staff to make the most effective possible contribution to the aims and objectives of their Faculty/Centre/Department and to the University as a whole.

This dual approach will best ensure the development of a flexible and well-motivated workforce, proactive in achieving the University's corporate goals.

Principles

The following principles inform this policy:

1   The University will ensure the maintenance and active promotion of equal opportunities in all its staff development provision. Access to appropriate staff development is in principle available to all staff. However, this principle does not imply automatic right of access to particular activities, or within specified periods of time.

2   All staff are expected and encouraged to participate in staff development activities aimed at improving the effectiveness and efficiency of the University's operations. Involvement in particular staff development activities is generally voluntary. However, attendance at certain activities will at times be a requirement for the allocation of certain duties and/or for all staff in one category or work area. It is expected that staff will cooperate with such requirements.

3   The University aims to ensure, within reasonable resource restraints, that staff have the maximum possible opportunity to engage in staff development activities. To this end an enhanced staff development budget has been made available under the Investors in People initiative.

4   Staff development aims to encourage the commitment of all staff in working towards excellence in the University's core functions of education and research, and excellence in the full range of support functions.

5   Staff development encompasses and encourages as wide a variety as possible of different types of activity, ranging from attendance at relevant courses, schemes of study and conferences, through undertaking self-directed study and research projects, to participation in cross-institutional working groups.

6   Staff development activities draw on the knowledge and skills of the University's staff as far as possible, with respect to both individuals who lead activities and those participating in the process.

7   Staff development is needs-driven rather than led by availability of provision.

This involves a proactive as well as a responsive approach.

8   Staff development involves a cycle of activity: planning, delivery, monitoring and evaluation. The results of evaluation are taken into account and acted upon for the next stage of the cycle.

B: Current structure and means of implementation

Responsibility

Responsibility for staff development is currently distributed in the following way:

i)   Individual responsibility
      Ultimate responsibility for the development of work-related skills and knowledge rests with each member of staff. Equally, all staff are expected not only to undertake initial developmental activities but also to continue to be active and responsive in identifying and meeting their own further needs. Where appropriate, they are expected to share their own work-related expertise so that the benefits they bring to the University and to other staff are maximised.

ii)   Managerial responsibility
      It is the responsibility of each manager to help in the identification of the developmental needs of their staff both individually and as a group, and for ensuring that these needs are appropriately addressed. The Appraisal system is an important part of this process. Managers undertake for their area an annual audit of staff development activity during the year and provide a statement of objectives for the following year.

      Managers of Faculties/Centres/Departments share responsibility with leaders of central staff development, for the provision of staff development activities and opportunities for their own staff and functions.

      Managers should ensure that the needs of staff employed short-term, part-time or as contract researchers, are addressed on an equitable basis.

      Managers are also expected to support the overall staff development programme by encouraging and facilitating involvement of their staff, whether as participants, organisers or activity leaders. In cases where groups or individual staff have expertise of particular relevance to the University's needs, managers are expected to play their part in ensuring that this is extended to others through relevant provision.

      In all these aspects managers act in collaboration with senior managers and with the central staff development service.

iii) Institutional responsibility
      At an institutional level the Pro Vice-Chancellor (Academic Staffing and Services) is responsible for the staff development of academic staff and the Secretary and Registrar for the staff development of support staff.

iv)   The Staff Development Unit

The Staff Development Unit (SDU) is responsible for providing a central institution-wide staff development service for all categories of staff. The SDU is part of the Personnel Department and is headed by the Director of Personnel.

v) Specialist Functions

Certain specialist areas of the University, such as the Academic Quality office and National Vocational Qualifications Development (NVQ) Unit, are responsible for institution-wide staff development for that function in collaboration with the SDU. Thus the NVQ Development Unit will ensure and coordinate opportunities for all staff to achieve relevant NVQs/GNVQs.

Implementation

This staff development policy is currently implemented through the following mechanisms:

1 Identification of needs

a) Organisational needs

Institutional objectives for staff development are formulated for the Strategic Plan and updated annually by senior management, including the Pro Vice-Chancellor (Academic Staffing and Services) and the Secretary and Registrar. These objectives take account of external and internal influences and prioritise major areas for staff development for the whole range of University activity, including, for example, teaching and learning, information technology and external profile.

At a local level information from a variety of sources, including for example the Appraisal and Student Feedback systems, is considered in the context of the University's strategic aims and objectives and of existing local priorities. Staff development plans for all Faculties, Centres, Departments and specialist functions are then prepared by the relevant managers, in liaison with those responsible for staff development centrally, including senior management and the SDU. Plans are expected to address all major functions relevant to the area in question.

b) Individual needs

The annual Appraisal system is one of the main ways in which individual staff development needs are recognised. The system ensures that all staff review their own developmental needs in the light of the aims and objectives of the University and of their Faculty/Centre/Department, and that they have an individual interview with their manager once annually, leading to the preparation and/or updating of a personal Action Plan. Following production of all Action Plans for their area each manager puts together a resume of staff development needs for that group. Resumes are made available for central planning undertaken by senior management in collaboration with the SDU.

2 Central provision – Staff Development Unit

The SDU offers a comprehensive generic service for all staff; liaises with and offers support to areas of the University in organising and providing for their own specialist needs; and acts in collaboration with other areas in extending their professional expertise across the University. SDU provision will in some cases complement and extend local provision, and in other cases will lead it: as, for example, in institutional induction and preparation for new staff in teaching methods.

The SDU organises a well-advertised programme of staff development opportunities for all staff. Members of the SDU also work collaboratively with staff across the University on an individual and group basis.

The work of the SDU is arranged under two main heads: provision for educational development (under the Head of Learning Development) and provision for general employment-related development, including the Investors in People initiative (under the Head of Training and Investors Coordinator).

The unit undertakes a thorough monitoring and evaluation of its work. An annual audit and report of its activity is prepared by the SDU for Academic Board and senior management.

i) Employment-related activity

    The Head of Training is responsible for providing centrally organised training and development for all categories of staff in generic employment-related skills, for example, induction to UH, time management, customer care, presentation skills, management related development. This also includes supporting groups of staff in team-working activities, especially linking in to IIP.

ii) Educational development

    The Head of Learning Development, is responsible for providing leadership and support to all relevant staff groups in the development of teaching and learning methods and personal skills, and associated staff development. This includes support for new staff such as the Professional Development Programme in Teaching and Learning in Higher Education and the Mentorship Programme. The Head of Learning Development also undertakes educational development activities and chairs the institution-wide Learning Development Network, set up to continue Enterprise in Higher Education themes. The Network is a sub-committee of the Learning and Teaching Committee, acts as its 'practitioner' arm and has a strong staff development element.

iii) Investors in People

    Through its commitment to the Investors in People standard, the University publicly affirms its belief that its staff and their development are vital to the organisation's success. In order to attain and retain the standard the University must satisfy all four Investors principles: commitment, planning, action and evaluation. Staff development is the key activity throughout. The Investors Coordinator operates from within the SDU. Investors Action Plans are prepared by an external consultant, following discussion with staff and managers. Implementation is a local responsibility, under the leadership of the relevant Dean or Director of Centre.

3 Funding

Staff development budgets are enhanced as part of the Investors in People programme. Funds are distributed according to a formula based on number and category of staff. Academic staff development budgets are devolved to Deans of Faculty, who supplement central funds with additional income earned by the Faculty from short courses and consultancy. Funds for staff development of support staff are also devolved to the relevant Dean of Faculty or Director of Centre.

In addition to covering direct costs for staff development activities, the budget may be used where appropriate for funding temporary cover while staff are engaged in staff development activities.

For events and other activities arranged by the SDU, financial expenditure is partly recouped from the relevant Faculty or Centre through a system of internal recharge.

University fees for part-time award bearing courses (ie degrees, certificates, CATS points) are waived for UH staff, including retired staff. There is no charge to the Faculty's/Centre's budget in this case. Additionally, the Associate Colleges will consider offering a 50% discount on a range of their other courses. However, both UH and Associate College commercial short courses are charged at the full rate and funds for these need to be provided through the Faculty's/Centre's own staff development budget.

C Strategic objectives

Strategic Objectives are published annually in the University's Strategic Plan.

June 1996

UNIVERSITY OF HERTFORDSHIRE

STAFF DEVELOPMENT POLICY

C: Strategic objectives for 1996–7

Institutional priorities for staff development during the academic year 1996–7 will be particularly focused on:

1   ensuring progress towards the achievement of the IIP award;

2 supporting preparation for Quality Assessment visits through facilitating and sharing of information, ideas and good practice;

3 raising the profile of the teaching and learning function across the University;

4 supporting and enhancing the University's research activities;

5 clarification of the University's policy and strategy on career development, particularly for support staff;

6 strengthening management development provision;

7 supporting the introduction and use of new technology in all areas of the University's operation, in accordance with the University's Information Systems Strategy;

8 furthering involvement in relevant NVQ/GNVQ opportunities.

Extracts from a Questionnaire on the First Year of the Professional Development Programme (PDP) (in Teaching And Learning In HE) Scheme

INSTRUCTIONS

This questionnaire contains questions on the courses you have taken, the lecturers who have taught you and the general experiences of your year. Please read through the questions and answer them carefully. Most of the questions ask you to respond with a letter from A to E:

A = strongly agree B = agree C = uncertain D = disagree E = strongly disagree

DO NOT MARK THE QUESTIONNAIRE: USE THE OMR ANSWER FORM

Use only the pencil provided. Strike through the letters clearly and carefully. Rub out any mistakes thoroughly with the eraser provided.

Put your course code and year, eg PSY1 in the box marked 'subject' on the top of the form.

A sheet of paper is also provided for any comments that you may wish to make.

Please work on your own. It is your individual opinions that we want to measure.

The questionnaire is anonymous so feel free to say what you really think. Please be constructive in your comments, as far as possible. Your replies will help us modify and improve students' experience at the University of Hertfordshire.

THE QUESTIONNAIRE

PART B

SCHEME EXPERIENCE QUESTIONNAIRE

The purpose of this questionnaire is to collect participants' opinions of the learning experience.

Please note that the 'scheme' will be your scheme overall as far as you have experienced it; the 'course' is a particular subject with a particular modular value.

This questionnaire is one which is widely used in research into learning in higher education. The questions are based on comments that students have often made about their experiences of higher education teaching. They have been specially chosen to reflect aspects of courses that are generally important across a wide range of disciplines.

How to answer

Simply circle the letter beside each statement that most accurately reflects your view.

a   means you definitely agree (//)
b   means that you agree, but with reservations (/)
c   means that you are not sure or that it doesn't apply(?)
d   means that you tend to disagree (x)
e   means that you definitely disagree (xx)

(**Note:** questions only included in this appendix)

---

41. It's always easy here to know the standard of work expected of you.
42. There are few opportunities to choose the particular areas you want to study.
43. The teaching staff on the courses motivate participants to do their best work.
44. The workload is too heavy.
45. Staff frequently give the impression that they haven't anything to learn from participants.
46. You usually have a clear idea of where you are going and what's expected of you.
47. Staff put a lot of time into commenting on participant's work.
48. To do well on this scheme all you really need is a good memory.
49. The scheme seems to encourage us to develop our own academic interests as far as possible.
50. It seems to me that the syllabuses try to cover too many topics.
51. Participants have a great deal of choice over how they are going to learn.
52. Staff seem more interested in testing what we have memorised than what we have understood.

53. It's often hard to discover what's expected of you in the courses.
54. We are generally given enough time to understand the things we have to learn.
55. The staff make a real effort to understand difficulties participants may be having with their work.
56. Participants are given a lot of choice in the work they have to do.
57. Staff normally give helpful feedback on how you are doing.
58. Our tutors are extremely good at explaining things to us.
59. The aims and objectives of the courses are not made very clear.
60. Tutors work hard to make their subjects interesting to participants.
61. Too many staff ask us questions just about facts.
62. There's a lot of pressure on you as a participant on this scheme.
63. Feedback on participant work is usually provided ONLY in the form of marks and grades.
64. We often discuss with our tutors how we are going to learn in the courses.
65. Staff show no real interest in what participants have to say.
66. It would be possible to get through these courses just by working hard around assessment times.
67. This scheme really tries to get the best out of its participants.
68. There's very little choice in this scheme in the ways you are assessed.
69. The staff make it clear right from the start what they expect from participants.
70. The sheer volume of work to be got through in the courses means that you can't comprehend it all thoroughly.

Extracts from EHE Quinquennial Review for the University of Hertfordshire

9 STAFF DEVELOPMENT

a) The progress of Staff Development

Academic staff development was not originally seen as one of the prime focuses of the programme and has not been one of the key themes, but rather a means to an end. Even so, one of the specific objectives addressed this area, stating that 'we will undertake a major staff development programme to develop appropriate skills in academic staff'. As the programme got underway the crucial importance of staff development became better recognised, for both training and development in new areas and also as essential support to enable the necessary personal and institutional change. Staff development has probably been the single most important factor in creating the new Enterprise culture.

Staff development covers a range of formal and informal learning situations, such as secondments, conferences, courses, networking and individual learning. Generally, though, only formal learning opportunities are recorded as such, and recorded data is mainly made up of reported events attended. Yet clearly learning derived from such events will be only a fraction of that achieved. It is obvious that looking at our figures for staff development will give both a very considerable underestimate and a distorted view of staff learning and development in general. Also a good proportion of Enterprise-related staff development events are offered by and attended by staff within their own School but are not seen as part of the programme and hence not recorded.

Despite all these factors the quantitative data for staff development is extremely healthy. From a head-count of 190 academic staff involved in one or more events during the first year of the programme the figures rose to 718 in the last full year. Similarly, the total hours spent in formal Enterprise staff development were 1,560 in the first year, rising to 8,710 in the last full year. Over the five year period the total time expenditure works out at 4,150 staff days of formal learning time.

As part of this, more than 120 staff have attended one of the 'Learning in Groups' residential courses. This is nearly a quarter of all academic staff in Enterprise contract areas. As this course is voluntary and requires being away from home for four days this suggests widespread commitment to Enterprise development. The extent of this commitment is also suggested in the increased number of staff choosing to extend their INSET courses with MA's and other teaching and learning qualifications.

b) Staff Development Review

A major review of Enterprise staff development was undertaken in February 1993. The report concluded that the existing programme was working positively overall. All Enterprise-funded events were evaluated, some (all those led by the Central Unit) very fully by means of participant feedback and evaluative reports. The general picture identified was that events and courses were well received, most were well attended and as measured through outcomes and subsequent activity were clearly bearing fruit.

Action points suggested by the report included the need for more coherent planning. An improved programme was subsequently drawn up. This included the outline of a new model, with a list of essential prerequisites for effective staff development in an area of rapid change, plus strategy, aims and roles for the programme. This model is now available to inform the work of the new Staff Development Unit, established as part of the continuation strategy.

As a result of the staff development review three things became, and remain, clear issues for future action. First, that the network approach is the right one. If Enterprise themes are to progress with maximum effectiveness in the post-funding period it will need to be through a continued and extended network. Hence the Learning Development Network.

Second, the present rate of change in HE is such that it threatened to overtake us even with the benefit of Enterprise. Academic staff development therefore becomes even more of a priority than hitherto if we are to continue to deliver quality courses. Academic Audit, Quality Assessment and the Investors in People programme will inevitably result in an increased need for staff development and again, an academic network is needed to deliver this. Lastly, change often involves personal threat to the individuals undertaking it, especially change on the scale we must now envisage. Maximum support and sensitivity are therefore needed in both the model used in staff development and the personal approach to the individuals who will deliver that programme.

10 EVALUATION AND MONITORING

a) Monitoring: procedures and evidence

The Central Unit set up and maintained systems for collecting quantitative evidence such as that required for performance indicators. For this purpose, 'Activity Reports' were an important source of information throughout the programme. These were structured proformas returned by staff to the Central Unit, giving factual details of Enterprise activities and including an evaluation section. This system worked well in some ways, particularly as a convenient source of quantitative data. However, some staff were more comfortable with the paperwork than others and their efficiency was variable.

For a number of reasons the feedback systems as a whole resulted in more accurate and complete reporting of one-off activities than of ongoing and embedded activities. This meant that the figures for our performance indicators were not properly cumulative, in that they mainly represented activities introduced during the current year. Hence we consistently under-reported. As we neared the end of the project this became increasingly noticeable. Although identified relatively early on this difficulty did prove intractable, especially as getting information on this scale depended to a large extent on voluntary reporting.

As the aim of Enterprise at UH has been to embed the initiative into the 'seamless robe' of the students' experience, and the name 'Enterprise' was by no means always used, so it was impossible to separate out what was due to Enterprise and what was not. Tracking became progressively more difficult as the project matured. As our independent Evaluator observed, there were always some staff who were reluctant to bring their own efforts, even where due to or influenced by the initiative, into the Enterprise arena in case they lost control or credit. This has been a further significant cause of under-reporting.

The need for more reliable data than obtainable through voluntary systems was behind the three Enterprise Audits: the Initial Audit undertaken in 1989–90, which provided 'baseline' mainly quantitative information, the Mid-Programme Audit of 1991–92 and the Final Audit of 1994. The report of this last is reproduced in full in Appendix IV; it includes a comparison of the final year's results with those of the two previous Audits, thus giving a good overview of the way Enterprise activity has spread across the university with time.

As might be expected, overall we also have much more reliable evidence of the specific effects of the programme and activity as such than for general effects and actual progress. This latter information has been obtained mainly through our evaluation procedures.

b) Evaluation

Evaluation has been a continuous process, the evidence for it coming in various forms and from various sources, including quantitative and qualitative monitoring data, reflective analysis, anecdotes and informed opinion drawn from students, staff, employers and others. Some comes from non-Enterprise sources, such as questionnaires on the student experience of teaching and learning, School academic committee reports and so on.

As mentioned earlier, for the first three years of the project we had an independent Local Evaluator from NICEC. This arrangement was very advantageous to the programme, and the outcomes of her work were much appreciated. The one major disadvantage was that it allowed the process of evaluation and the responsibility for it to be seen as largely external to those involved in the programme. In addition, this being a highly devolved project, despite our best efforts there has been a tendency for an overview to be visible from the centre, but not so easily seen by those in the Schools. Opportunities for the Schools to learn and change as a result of each other's evaluation were relatively few in the first half of the programme.

With the demise of NICEC in Summer 1992 the opportunity was taken to relocate the evaluation function internally. As we moved towards the post-funding phase it seemed vital that evaluation of Enterprise-type activities should become an integrated process in the university, part of the regular quality cycle and firmly embedded in the on-going culture of a learning organisation. While the need for monitoring and for evaluation for accountability and management purposes would disappear with the end of funding, the need for the developmental role of evaluation would persist. The shift, then, was seen as essential preparation for the future.

From September 1992 the Enterprise Director took responsibility for overall evaluation and for liaising with the Schools in deciding the detailed operation of the system within their area. Schools Tutors/Coordinators and Central Service representatives were responsible for carrying out that system and for providing information to the Central Unit. This proved effective in promoting increased ownership of the evaluation function. Joint activities enabled participants to learn from one another's sometimes very different School culture and progress. The intention is that the internal process now established will be continued in future by the relevant LDN members, though for different purposes.

The internal process has included the development of ways of describing the culture change through, as one example, looking at the language in common use across the university. Some of the outcomes of this approach have been reported above under the various specific objectives.

References

Barnett, R (1990) *The Idea of Higher Education*, SRHE and Open University Press, Buckingham.

Barnett, R (1992) *Improving Higher Education: Total Quality Care*, SRHE, London.

Becher, T (1989) *Academic Tribes and Territories*, SRHE and Open University Press, Buckingham.

Bernthal, P (1995) Evaluation that Goes the Distance, *American Journal of Training & Development*, vol 49, 9 January 1995, p 41.

Bilham, T (1989) *Staff Development for Continuing Education*, DES, London.

Blackwell and McLean, 1996.

Blake, R R and Mouton, J S (1964) *The Managerial Grid*, Gulf Publishing, Houston, TX.

Bramley, P (1996) *Evaluating Training Effectiveness* (2nd edn), McGraw-Hill, New York.

Brown, S and Knight, P (1994) *Assessing Learners in Higher Education*, Kogan Page, London.

Burge, S E and Tannock, J D T (1994) A Practical Approach to Implementing Quality Management in Higher Education – a discussion document prepared by the EPC working party on quality assurance, *Engineering Professors' Council Occasional Paper*, no 7, December 1994.

Burgoyne, J (1992) Creating a Learning Organisation, *RSA Journal* **140**, April, 321–36.

Cameron, K (1980) 'Critical Questions in Assessing Organisational Effectiveness' in *Organisational Dynamics*, Autumn 1980, pp 66–80.

Cameron, W B (1963) *Informal Sociology: A Casual Introduction to Sociological Thinking*, Random House, New York.

REFERENCES

CNAA (1992) *The Management of Academic Quality in Institutions of Higher Education*, CNAA, London.

Cox, B (1994) *Practical Pointers for University Teachers*, Kogan Page, London.

Crosby, P B (1984) *Quality Without Tears*, McGraw-Hill, New York.

Cryer, P (ed) (1992) *Effective Learning and Teaching in Higher Education*, USDU (now UCoSDA), Sheffield.

CVCP (1996) *Response to the National Committee of Inquiry into Higher Education*, CVCP, London.

Deming, E W (1986) *Out of The Crisis*, MIT, Boston, MA.

Drucker, P F (1993) *Managing in Turbulent Times*, Butterworth-Heinemann, Oxford.

Easterby-Smith, M (1994) *Evaluation Of Management Education, Training and Development* (2nd edn), Gower, Aldershot.

Entwistle, N (1992) *The Impact of Teaching on Learning Outcomes in Higher Education*, USDU (now UCoSDA), Sheffield.

Entwistle, N J and Tait, H (1990) Approaches To Learning, Evaluations Of Teaching And Preferences For Contrasting Learning Environments, *Higher Education*, 19.

Erwin, T D (1991) *Assessing Student Learning and Development*, Jossey Bass, San Francisco, CA.

Feigenbaum, A V (1986) *Total Quality Control*, McGraw-Hill, New York.

Fry, S (1992) *Paperweight*, Heinemann, Oxford.

Goldstein, I L (1993) *Training in Organisations*, Brooks-Cole, Monterey, Belmont and Pacific Grove, CA.

HEFCE (1995a) Circular 26/95 *Quality Assessment between October 1996 and September 1998*, HEFCE, Bristol.

HEQC (1995) *A Quality Assurance Framework for Guidance and Learner Support in Higher Education: the Guidelines*, HEQC, London.

HEQC (1996) *Guidelines on Quality Assurance*, HEQC, London.

Heywood, J (1989) *Assessment in Higher Education*, Wiley, Chichester.

Hinrichs, J R (1976) Personnel Training in Dunnette (ed) *Handbook of Organisational and Industrial Psychology*, Rand McNally, Chicago, IL.

Jackson, T (1989) *Evaluation: Relating Training to Business Performance*, Kogan Page, London.

REFERENCES

Juran, J M (1988) *Juran on Planning For Quality*, Free Press, New York.

Kearns, P and Miller, T (1996) *Training Measurement and Evaluation*, Technical Communications Publishing Ltd., Hitchin, Herts.

Kirkpatrick, D L (1958/9) Techniques for Evaluating Training Programmes, *Journal for the American Society of Training Directors* 13, November, 14, February (the journal is now *Training and Development*).

Kolb, D and Lewis, L H (1986) Facilitating Experiential Learning: observations and reflections, *New Directions for Continuing Education* **30**, June, 99–107.

Laycock, M J (1996) *Quality Improvement in Learning and Teaching Handbook*, University of East London, London.

Lee, R (1996) The Pay Forward View of Training, *People Management*, February.

Legge, K (1984) *Evaluating Planned Organisational Change*, Academic Press, London.

Lodge, D (1995) *Therapy*, Penguin, London.

Mayo, A and Lank, E (1994) *The Power of Learning: A Guide to Learning Independently*, Open University Press, Buckingham.

Middlehurst, R (1993) *Leading Academics*, SRHE and Open University, Buckingham.

Mills, D Q and Friesen, B (1992) The Learning Organisation, *European Management Journal* **10**, 2, June, 146–56.

Murphy, J (1992) Quality University Management Programmes, *International Journal of Educational Management*, vol 6, no. 2, pp 18–25.

National Committee of Inquiry into Higher Education (NCIHE) (1997) *Higher Education In The Learning Society. Report of the Committee*, HMSO, Norwich.

Nevo (1986) New Directions in Educational Evaluation in House, E (ed) Falmer Press, London.

Newble, D and Cannon, R (1991) *A Handbook for Teachers in Universities and Colleges: a Guide to Improving Teaching Methods* (2nd edn), Kogan Page, London.

O'Neill, M and Pennington, G (1992) *Evaluating Teaching and Courses from an Active Learning Perspective*, USDU/CVCP, Sheffield.

Partington, P (1994) *Human Resources Management and Development in Higher Education*, Paper presented at Quinquennial Conference of European Rectors, Budapest, UCoSDA, Sheffield.

Patton, M Q (1997) *Utilisation Focused Evaluation* (3rd edn), Sage, London.

REFERENCES

Pedler, M, Burgoyne, J G and Boydell T (1991) *The Learning Company: A Strategy for Sustainable Growth*, McGraw-Hill, New York.

Philips, J J (1991) *Handbook of Training Evaluation and Measurement Methods* (2nd edn), Kogan Page, London.

Piper, D W (1993) *Quality Management in Universities*, University of Queensland, Australian Government Publishing Service, Queensland, Australia.

Pirsig, R M (1974) *Zen And The Art Of Motorcycle Maintenance*, Bodley Head, London.

Ramsden, P (1991) A Performance Indicator of Teaching Quality in Higher Education: the Course Experience Questionnaire, *Studies in Higher Education*, 16, 2.

Ramsden, P (1992) Learning to Teach in Higher Education, *Research Papers in Education*, 4: 22–56.

Rix, A, Parkinson, R and Gaunt, R (1994) *Investors in People: A Qualitative Study of Employers*, Research Series Report No. 21, January, Research Strategy Branch, Employment Department, Moorfoot, Sheffield.

Senge, P (1990) *The Fifth Discipline: The Art and Practice of the Learning Organisation*, Doubleday, London.

Skinner, B F (1964) Education Is What Survives When What Has Been Learnt Has Been Forgotten, *New Scientist*, May 1984.

Stace, D A and Dunphy, D C (1991) Beyond Traditional Paternalistic And Developmental Approaches To Organisational Change And Human Resource Strategies, *The International Journal of Human Resource Management*, 2, 3, 263–83.

Stake, R E (1975) *Evaluating The Arts in Education: A Responsive Approach*, Charles E Merrill, Columbus, OH.

Taguchi, G (1985) *What Is Total Quality Control? The Japanese Way*, Prentice-Hall, Englewood Cliffs, NJ.

Taylor, P and Thackwray, R (1996) *Investors in People Explained* (revised 2nd edn), Kogan Page, London.

Taylor, P and Thackwray, R (1997) *Managing for Investors in People*, Kogan Page, London.

Thackwray, B (1994) University Staff: A Worthwhile Investment? in P T Knight (ed) *University-wide Change, Staff and Curriculum Development*, Staff and Educational Development Association (SEDA), Birmingham, SEDA Paper 83, May, 71–77.

Thackwray, R (1996) *The Revised Indicators Explained*, Briefing Paper 33, Sheffield.

REFERENCES

Thackwray, R (1996) *The QILT Education Report*, University of East London, London.

UCoSDA (1994) *A Compendium of Principles for Developing and Enhancing Student Learning*, UCoSDA, Sheffield.

UCoSDA (1994) *Continuing Professional Development (CPD) of Staff in Higher Education (HE): Informing Strategic Thinking*, UCoSDA, Sheffield.

UCoSDA (1995) *Training Programme for HEFCE Assessors*, UCoSDA/CVCP, Sheffield.

UCoSDA (1996) *Response to The National Committee of Inquiry into Higher Education*, UCoSDA, Sheffield.

UCoSDA (1996) *The Revised Indicators Explained*, Briefing paper 33, April, UCoSDA, Sheffield.

Warr, P, Bird, M and Rackham, N (1970) *Evaluation of Management Training*, Gower Press, London.

Webb, G (1996) *Understanding Staff Development*, SRHE/Open University, Buckingham.

Yorke, M (1996) *Indicators of Programme Quality*, HEQC, London.

Index

References in italic indicate figures and tables.